GREAT WORDS of THE GOSPEL

STUDIES IN THE MAJOR THEMES OF SALVATION

KEN CHANT

GREAT WORDS of THE GOSPEL

STUDIES IN THE MAJOR THEMES OF SALVATION

KEN CHANT

Third Edition – 2012

ISBN 978-1-61529-065-9

Copyright © 2012 Ken Chant

Vision Publishing
1672 Main St. E 109
Ramona, CA 92065
1-800-9-VISION
www.booksbyvision.com

All rights reserved worldwide

No part of the book may be reproduced in any manner whatsoever without written permission of the author except in brief quotations embodied in critical articles of reviews.

A NOTE ON GENDER

It is unfortunate that the English language does not contain an adequate generic pronoun (especially in the singular number) that includes without bias both male and female. So *"he, him, his, man, mankind,"* with their plurals, must do the work for both sexes. Accordingly, wherever it is appropriate to do so in the following pages, please include the feminine gender in the masculine, and vice versa.

FOOTNOTES

A work once fully referenced will thereafter be noted either by "ibid" or "op. cit."

CONTENTS

PREFACE: SO GREAT SALVATION..........................5

ADDENDUM: MODELS OF SALVATION...................... 9

CHAPTER ONE: REGENERATION 13

CHAPTER TWO - PART ONE: JUSTIFICATION 25

CHAPTER TWO - PART TWO: JUSTIFICATION 43

CHAPTER THREE: REDEMPTION..........................59

CHAPTER FOUR: PREDESTINATION 75

CHAPTER FIVE: SANCTIFICATION 97

CHAPTER SIX: POSITION.................................119

CHAPTER SEVEN: LEGALISM 131

CHAPTER EIGHT: LIBERTY 151

ADDENDUM ONE: THE PIERCED EAR 173

ADDENDUM TWO: THEORIES OF ATONEMENT...........179

ABBREVIATIONS

Abbreviations commonly used for the books of the Bible are

Genesis	Ge	Habakkuk	Hb
Exodus	Ex	Zephaniah	Zp
Leviticus	Le	Haggai	Hg
Numbers	Nu	Zechariah	Zc
Deuteronomy	De	Malachi	Mal
Joshua	Js		
Judges	Jg		
Ruth	Ru	Matthew	Mt
1 Samuel	1 Sa	Mark	Mk
2 Samuel	2 Sa	Luke	Lu
1 Kings	1 Kg	John	Jn
2 Kings	2 Kg	Acts	Ac
1 Chronicles	1 Ch	Romans	Ro
2 Chronicles	2 Ch	1 Corinthians	1 Co
Ezra	Ezr	2 Corinthians	2 Co
Nehemiah	Ne	Galatians	Ga
Esther	Es	Ephesians	Ep
Job	Jb	Philippians	Ph
Psalm	Ps	Colossians	Cl
Proverbs	Pr	1 Thessalonians	1 Th
Ecclesiastes	Ec	2 Thessalonians	2 Th
Song of Songs	Ca *	1 Timothy	1 Ti
Isaiah	Is	2 Timothy	2 Ti
Jeremiah	Je	Titus	Tit
Lamentations	La	Philemon	Phm
Ezekiel	Ez	Hebrews	He
Daniel	Da	James	Ja
Hosea	Ho	1 Peter	1 Pe
Joel	Jl	2 Peter	2 Pe
Amos	Am	1 John	1 Jn
Obadiah	Ob	2 John	2 Jn
Jonah	Jo	3 John	3 Jn
Micah	Mi	Jude	Ju
Nahum	Na	Revelation	Re

Ca is an abbreviation of *Canticles*, a derivative of the Latin name of the *Song of Solomon*, which is sometimes also called the *Song of Songs*.

Note: scripture translations are my own, unless otherwise noted.

PREFACE:

SO GREAT SALVATION

This is a book about salvation. Not just any salvation. But that

> *GREAT SALVATION . . . which was declared first by the Lord, and then was confirmed to us by those who heard him, while God added his own testimony through signs and wonders, various miracles, and gifts of the Holy Spirit (He 2:3,4).*

In the language of the New Testament, to be *saved* means two things: first, to be brought into a *place* of *"safety"*; and second, to be brought into a *state* of *"soundness"*. One who is *saved* has escaped from the stormy winds of the wrath of God, and has been given access to heaven's healing balm. Salvation brings us into the Father's pleasant and secure haven; and there we also find a grace that can make us whole. Refugees from sin become sons of Royalty!

In other words, this salvation gives the believer access to everything God has provided for humanity by the sacrificial death of his Son, Jesus Christ, at Calvary. It includes: pardon for every sin; adoption into the Father's family; victory over Satan's power; healing of body, mind, and spirit; a complete and free gift of righteousness; an abundant provision for every need; peace of mind; a guarantee of resurrection; and a destiny to reign as a prince when Christ comes.

How great this salvation is! It leaves no part of my life untouched. Because of the grace of God in Christ I can boast that

(1) *I am saved from the PENALTY of sin*

> This is the *past tense* of salvation, and it speaks of the complete freedom from condemnation that is God's gift to all who place their wholehearted confidence in Christ as Saviour and Lord (see Ep 2:4-5; Ro 6:23).

(2) *I am being saved from the POWER of sin*

This is the *present tense* of salvation, and it speaks of an ever-increasing victory over sin that is the experience of all true believers; it also describes the Christian's steady growth in Christ-likeness.

(3) *I am about to be saved from the PRESENCE of sin*

This is the *future tense* of salvation, and it speaks of the great hope that lies before us in the second advent of Christ - for on that day the church will be raptured, and the saints of God will enter into the magnificent inheritance their Lord has bequeathed them.

Yesterday, today, and tomorrow! All are embraced by this great salvation!

The purpose of this book is to mine the riches of salvation by digging into some of the key words scripture uses to describe its benefits. Hence the title, *"Great Words of the Gospel."* So you will not find here a comprehensive search through salvation; rather, I am content to explore just a few of the brighter veins of gospel ore.

THEOLOGIANS CALL IT "SOTERIOLOGY"

In a more orthodox study program, I might have called these lessons *"The Doctrine of Salvation;"* or, with a greater display of erudition, *"Soteriology"*. But then the treatment of the subject would have been formal, self-consistent, and free of any ambiguities. It would have harmonised with one or other of the various systematic theologies the church has coughed up over the centuries - but it might not have borne much resemblance to scripture.

The quotation that follows, from James Stewart, will explain what I mean -

> (Much harm has been done by) the tendency, on the part of Roman Catholics and Protestants alike, to systematise Paul's teaching into elaborate *"plans of salvation"*, to the details and order of which the experience of believers has been required to conform - the tendency, in other words, to stereotype the grace of God . . . Moreover, the logical conclusion of any plan of redemption worked out

after this pattern, in elaborate successive steps and stages, must be the reducing of Christian experience to a drab, colourless uniformity; and it is hard to believe that the God whose Spirit is like the wind, blowing where it listeth, ever intended anything of the kind . . . Nor is it sound to draw a hard-and-fast line, as is often done, between the various elements in Christian experience, to posit a hiatus, as it were, between repentance and regeneration, or between conversion and forgiveness, or between justification and sanctification . . . Endless misconceptions have been caused by isolating the various elements in the Christian experience from one another, and assigning each its place on the chronological chart. [1]

The fact is, God's marvelous salvation is ultimately indescribable, it cannot finally be explained: *"Thanks be to God for his <u>inexpressible</u> gift!"* (2 Co 9:15). So I have not tried to present a systematic or formal treatise, nor even one free from anomalies or tensions. You will probably find as many of those problems in this book as you can in the New Testament!

The gospel message is so amazing, its treasures so inexhaustible, the apostles were obliged to use a score or more different analogies, some of them sharply contrasting, in their endeavours to portray the dazzling wonder of God's love. Thus, the church is the *"body"* of Christ, but also his *"bride"*; the blood of Jesus is a ransom, yet it also makes reconciliation; the cross provides atonement, yet is also an agent of propitiation; we are *"free-born"* children of God, but we are also *"adopted"*; and so on. [2]

John Stott drew attention to the same diversity -

---

[1] <u>A Man In Christ</u>, Hodder & Stoughton, London, 1972; pg. 9 ff.
[2] Another way to look at the same problem is to present the message of salvation in the form of various "models." I have been able to identify twelve such models, which are outlined in the *Addendum* at the end of this chapter.

> (Many evangelicals) behave as if God has given a series of precise formulae that we have to repeat more or less word for word, and certain images that we must invariably employ. This leads to bondage either to words or images, or both. Some evangelists lapse into the use of stale jargon, while others feel obliged on every occasion to mention *"the blood of Christ"*, or *"justification by faith"*, or *"the kingdom of God"*, or some other image. [3]

In contrast with that kind of dreary uniformity the apostles looked at this supreme theme of salvation from many different perspectives, using a startling variety of illustrations, a bewildering array of ideas. Yet in the end even they failed to measure the full height and depth, the width and breadth, of all that God has wrought for us in Christ. Eventually the ecstatic soul can only exclaim that this great salvation truly does surpass all human knowledge! (Ep 3:18-19)

For that reason, these lessons do not attempt a complete explanation of what the Bible means when it says *"believe and be saved"*; nor do they seek to present a comprehensive theory of how the cross has provided atonement for sin. If that had been my task, I would have despaired before I began. Theories and theologies abound, but not one of them has yet found universal acceptance among the churches.

Happily, my aspirations were more humble. I have been content to take only a few of the arresting and exciting words used by the NT writers, and to mirror in them the stunning splendour of God's amazing gift. But even in those few words there are wonders enough to keep the angels and the saints singing the glories of God forever!

---

[3] Christianity Today, Feb 6th, 1981; pg. 28.

ADDENDUM:

MODELS OF SALVATION

The gospel is one gospel and it offers a single great salvation; but like a beautiful diamond, this precious jewel shines with many colours and presents many different faces or we might say that the NT presents the gospel through various analogies or models I have been able to identify at least twelve such models in the NT –

(1) THE REGENERATIVE MODEL
- the key idea is a "new birth"
- sees salvation as a dynamic impartation of divine life (Jn 3:1-8)
- this is the main modern evangelical view, although it has not always been so emphasised
- it is uncommon in the Bible; it was never used by Jesus in public, but only in private to Nicodemus
- its weakness is its dependence upon a kind of religious experience that is common to virtually all major religions.

(2) THE REDEMPTIVE MODEL
- the key idea is "ransom"
- sees salvation as payment of a debt (Mt 20:28)
- includes also the idea of emancipation from slavery, about which could be asked: *"Who is paid?"* and, *"What is the price?"*

(3) THE DELIVERANCE MODEL
- the key idea is "rescue."

- sees salvation as an act of liberation from the grip of sin and Satan (Cl 1:13-14)

(4) THE SACERDOTAL MODEL
- the key idea is "atonement."
- sees salvation as a result of priestly sacrifice and intercession (He 7:23-28)
- churches that emphasise this concept tend to express it in their style of worship (a priesthood, liturgy, altar, etc.)
- indeed, all churches tend to display in their worship style the model of salvation that each one emphasises.

(5) THE CONTRACTUAL MODEL
- the key idea is "covenant."
- sees salvation as God and man honouring the terms of an indissoluble pact (Lu 22:20)
- within the framework of this model the direst warnings in the NT are given against falling back (cp. He 10:26-31)
- note the ferocity of God's dealings with Israel: they had sworn a solemn oath, thus bringing the nation into a special relationship with God of both blessing and cursing
- that is why we cannot do what the ungodly do, why they may be permitted to prosper while we are cut down.

(6) THE CONCILIATORY MODEL
- the key idea is "propitiation."
- sees salvation as the ending of a quarrel between God and man (1 Jn 4:10)
- it holds two ideas: placating the anger of God; and wooing a response from men and women.

(7) THE CORPORATE MODEL
- the key idea is "body."

- sees salvation as a social dynamic, offering safety through membership in the family of God (the church) (Ep 2:14-22; 3:6)
- includes the ideas of becoming part of the "body" of Christ, and of being adopted into the Father's family
- it is based upon the example of Israel, and leads to the doctrine of infant baptism

(8) THE SYNTHETIC MODEL
- the key idea is "union."
- sees salvation as a fusion of the believer with Christ (1 Jn 5:11-12)
- "synthesis" is the process by which various items are combined together to form a new whole; hence we come together "in Christ", and salvation is the result of our union with him.

(9) THE MESSIANIC MODEL
- the key idea is "kingdom."
- sees salvation as Christ's conquest of the kingdom of darkness (Cl 2:15).
- this is a common NT idea: that Christ has invaded this planet, overthrown Satan, liberated the devil's helpless victims, established his own universal dominion, and now invites us to share the spoils of his victorious war
- this emphasis is needed in the evangelical world, which has so concentrated on the sin-forgiving aspect of the gospel that its message has become etherealised, divorced from real life (compare the NT emphasis on exorcism, defeating the kingdom of darkness, and other acts of power).

(10) THE AFFILIATION MODEL
- the key idea is "adoption."
- sees salvation as God elevating the believer to the status of a son or daughter (Ga 4:4-7)

(11) THE POSITIONAL MODEL
- the key idea is "identification."
- sees salvation in terms of the believer's spiritual identification with Christ in his resurrection, ascension, and enthronement (Ep 2:4-6)

(12) THE FORENSIC MODEL
- the key idea is "justification."
- sees salvation as a legal transaction that secures our acquittal before the Judge (Ro 5:1)
- in particular is one of Paul's major themes
- it includes the ideas of: a substitute victim; legal satisfaction; acquittal through lack of evidence; forensic identification with Christ in his death.

All of those models are necessary to encompass the incredible height, breadth, and depth of the mercy God has shown us in Christ. It is spiritually unhealthy to focus upon one of them, to the exclusion of the others. The better your grasp of each of these models, the richer your Christian life will be.

CHAPTER ONE:
REGENERATION

One of the Bible's best known stories tells about Nicodemus, who came to Jesus late one night (Jn 3:1-9). It has a strange fascination, this furtive approach to Jesus, the Man from Nazareth, by Nicodemus, the Ruler from Jerusalem.

Nicodemus was a Pharisee. He was also a rich and powerful member of the supreme judicial body in ancient Jewry, the great Sanhedrin. Jesus called him a *"master"* in Israel, one of the top teachers of the nation. He was a brilliant and gifted man, a counsellor whose ministry and wisdom were widely sought. He had a deep understanding of scripture, and especially of the messianic prophecies. He believed that the ancient oracles were inspired by God, and he knew from his study of them that the time of Messiah's birth had already passed. He knew that the Messiah should now be a grown man, and he wondered if Jesus of Nazareth were indeed the Christ, the Anointed One, the Deliverer of Israel.

So Nicodemus enquired when he could find Jesus alone, then went to see him late one night. He came with his brilliant mind, his strong power of logic, and began to reason with the Lord -

> *Rabbi, we know that you are a teacher sent to us by God,*
> *for no one can work miracles like you do unless God is*
> *with him!*

But before Nicodemus could press any further into his argument, Christ interrupted him and struck at his real need. Bluntly, forcefully, Jesus told that prominent Jew: *"You must be born again!"*

At no time did Jesus speak words more arresting than those, especially when we see them in the light of the man at who first heard them -

> he was a ruler
> he was rich
> he was religious

> he revered the scriptures
> he was Israel's Teacher
> he believed in God
> he accepted the supernatural
> he respected Jesus

Yet Christ reckoned he was not saved! Nicodemus was cut off from the kingdom. He was not even a spiritual infant. He had not so much as reached the point of an initial *"birth"* into the family of God! Jesus was emphatic. The Pharisee could not even *begin* his spiritual pilgrimage until he had first experienced that *"new birth"*.

But what does this mean, to be *"born again"*?

THE NATURE OF THE NEW BIRTH

Christ spoke to Nicodemus about a new birth. He said, *"You must be born again."*

The Pharisee heard those words and immediately saw at least part of what Jesus meant. So he changed his approach, and earnestly asked, *"How can a man be born when he is old?"*

Nicodemus understood that Christ was demanding a *total life-change*.

But how can this be? How can life start anew? How can the past be eradicated? How can habits and a way of life formed over many years be so dramatically changed? Said Nicodemus, *"It would be easier to ask a man to re-enter his mother's womb and to be born a second time!"*

The Pharisee did see the startling significance of Jesus' words. With all his heart he longed that it might be so. Yet it seemed like an impossible dream. How can an old sin-weary man become like an innocent child?

That is a good question! What is this new birth? How does God make it happen?

REGENERATION DEFINED

The Bible uses various expressions to describe this experience: *"born again,"* *"born from above,"* *"born anew,"* *"born of the Spirit,"* and *"regeneration"* (Tit 3:5). That last word has become the technical expression by which the experience of the new birth is known, and it is the word I will use here.

But what does *"regeneration"* mean?

A good way to answer that question is to show what it does *not* mean -

To be *"regenerated"* or *"born again"* does *not* mean a mere reformation of life-style, nor does it stop with sorrow for sin, nor is it satisfied by becoming *"religious"*. The new birth is not found in some church ceremony; nor is it found in church membership. It does not consist of good works, no matter how sacrificial or noble.

A person can go through all the forms of church life and of religious observances, and yet remain unregenerate. That is made plain by the story of Nicodemus, who was a deeply religious and presumably God-fearing man; *yet he was not "born again"*.

People today are still relying on their social standing, or their Bible knowledge, or their intellectual belief in God, or their church activities, or their good works, to bring them eternal life.

But scripture is emphatic that no one, by personal skill, or effort, or goodness, can ever enter the kingdom of God. There is only one access, and that is through the process of regeneration - the spiritual counterpart of our natural birth. What other way can a baby enter the natural world except by way of the womb? What other way can a sinner enter the supernatural world except by way of the new birth?

REGENERATION CONFIRMED

Although Christ had explained what he meant by the demand, *"You must be born again,"* Nicodemus was still perplexed. He asked a second time, *"How can this be?"* (vs. 9). The Lord was surprised. He exclaimed, *"How can you be the Teacher of Israel, and yet not understand this?"*

Christ felt that Nicodemus, who held the high office of "Teacher" in Israel, should have remembered that the prophets had spoken about these things.

Nonetheless, Jesus patiently repeated himself: while no man can comprehend the mystery of the new birth, *all men may feel its power*. This mystery and this power Christ then confirmed by an illustration. He said -

> *The wind blows wherever it pleases, and you can hear the sound of it; but you don't know where it comes from*

> *nor where it goes; so is everyone who is born of the Spirit* (Jn 3:8).

Even today, despite their vast knowledge, meteorologists still do not really understand the way of the winds. For most of us it remains true: we cannot tell where the wind comes from nor where it will go. But while we may not understand the wind, we nevertheless feel its force, and use its energy constantly - to pump water, to drive ships across the ocean, to generate power, to cool our homes.

So it is with the new birth. No one is able to understand it; but all who will may experience its power to change their lives radically, to blot out the guilt of the past, to create an incredible new beginning, to bring them from time into eternity.

When Jesus spoke of water and wind to Nicodemus, he expected the learned Pharisee immediately to connect his words with the prophecies of the OT, notably those of *Ezekiel*. One passage in particular vividly portrays the wonderful results of being born of the Spirit - see *36:25-26; 37:9-10*.

Have *you* felt the flow of that living water in your soul? Have you allowed God to give you a new heart and a new spirit? Has the Breath of God breathed on you, turning you from death to life, and filling you with his grace and love?

How much we all need the experience Saul had -

> *The Spirit of the Lord will come upon you in power . . . and you will be changed into a different person!* (1 Sa 10:6)

For us, that process begins, and only can begin, with the new birth.

REGENERATION ANALYSED

There are certain essential components of the new birth. All who are truly born again have all of these things. These things put together are what make a person regenerate -

FAITH

> *Everyone who believes that Jesus is the Christ is born of God.* (1 Jn. 5:1)

Faith is the beginning, the middle, and the end of regeneration, as it is of everything to do with Christian life. It is simply impossible to please God if you are without faith (He 11:6). I will have more to say about this in the next chapter, on *Justification*.

CLEANSING

> *(God) saved us, not because we have done anything righteous, but out of his own great mercy, by washing us through regeneration and renewing us in the Holy Spirit* (Tit 3:5).

It should be noted that we have almost as little to do with our second birth as we had to do with our first. Certainly this is true as far as the impartation of life is concerned. It is by no act of ours that we came to natural life, and no deed of ours can bring us to spiritual life. It is all of God's mercy. Left to ourselves we were utterly ruined -

> *We ourselves once behaved like fools. We were disobedient, easily misled, slaves to many passions, servants of pleasure, devoting ourselves to anger and envy, hated by everyone and hating everyone* (vs. 3).

But if you have been born again then the Lord has also washed you clean of all such things.

QUICKENING

> *Put off your old nature, which once controlled the way you lived, thoroughly corrupted by lust and deceit, and be <u>renewed</u> in your innermost mind, putting on the <u>new nature</u>, which carries the likeness of God, made in true righteousness and holiness* (Ep 4:22-23; Cl 3:9-10).

NEW CREATION

> *Therefore, anyone who is in Christ, is a new creation, for the old life has passed away, and a new life has come* (2 Co 5:17). *For we are God's handiwork, created in Christ Jesus to do good things, which God has already planned for us, so that we might surely achieve them* (Ep 2:10).

The OT prophets predicted this new creation under the figure of "a new heart" *(see Ps 51:10; Je 31:33; Ez 11:19; etc.)*

RESURRECTION

> *The death Christ died he died to sin, once for all, but the life he lives he lives to God. In the same way, you too must consider yourselves dead to sin but alive to God in Christ Jesus* (Ro 6:10-11). *Once you were dead in your wrongdoing, but God has now made you alive together with Christ* (Cl 2:13). *Even though we were dead because of our wrongdoing (God) made us alive again together with Christ, and enthroned us with him in the heavenly places* (Ep 2:5-6).

To sum it up, there is a sparkling vitality associated with regeneration, a dynamic impartation of life, as real as that experienced in our physical birth. Admittedly, this divine life can become suppressed, people can become spiritual cripples, they may fail to live in the splendour of this new dimension - but its reality remains unchanged. The cleansing, the quickening, the renewal, the resurrection, contained in the new birth are always there, ready to be appropriated by the believing child of God.

THE NECESSITY OF THE NEW BIRTH

Jesus said -

> *I tell you solemnly, unless you are born of water and the Spirit, you cannot enter the kingdom of God. . . . Do not be surprised when I tell you again: "You must be born from above."* (Jn 3:3,7)

Then he laid down the reason for those strong injunctions -

> *That which is born of the flesh is flesh, and that which is born of the Spirit is spirit.* (vs. 6)

Across the ages of human history mankind has ever chosen the way of the flesh, not the way of the Spirit. Adam and Eve chose the fleshy tree of knowledge rather than the sacred tree of life, so God was compelled to pronounce the dread sentence of death upon them. Adam had been made a *"living soul"*, but when he fell the Lord said to him, *"You are dust, and to dust you shall return."* From a being whose predominant characteristic was spirit, he became a being whose predominant characteristic was flesh.

That sentence of death, that carnal disposition, has now been passed on to the entire human race. We are all born of the flesh, and we cannot, in this fleshy state, enter the kingdom of God. Hence the scripture says -

> *The natural man cannot receive anything that comes from the Spirit of God, for they seem like folly to him; nor can he understand them, because they must be spiritually discerned.* And again: *Flesh and blood cannot inherit the kingdom of God, neither can perishable things inherit the imperishable.* And again: *God is spirit, and those who worship him must worship in spirit and truth* (1 Co 2:14; 15:50; Jn. 4:24).

So you can see how absolutely necessary it is for a person to be born again. Only by the new birth can we receive eternal life and enter the kingdom of God. And this spiritual life can be received only through faith in the Lord Jesus Christ. Faith is the catalyst that brings us to an encounter with the Holy Spirit, who regenerates us, so that we are born into the heavenly realm just as surely as we were once born into the earthly realm.

The necessity of the new birth is emphasised in other places -

➢ The universal results of sin demand it -

Sin came into the world through one man and death followed after sin; therefore death spread throughout the world, because there are none who have not sinned *(Ro 5:12; see also 3:10-18,23; 6:23).*

➢ Unregenerate man is quite unable to understand or receive the gifts of God (1 Co 2:14).

➢ Without the new birth everything we do, every impulse and action, is defiled (Mk 7:21-23).

➢ Unless we are born again we have no escape from the judgment of God -

> *You were dead because of the trespasses and sins that once controlled your life, in which you followed the ways of the world . . . We all used to live among such people,*

> *gratifying the passions of our bodies, following the desires of our sinful nature, and so making ourselves, like the rest of mankind, the inheritors of God's anger (Ep 2:1-3; Is 59:2; Ro 1:18).*

HOW WE ARE BORN AGAIN

There are two sides to regeneration, the divine and the human. There are certain things God does, and certain things we must do -

THE DIVINE SIDE

On the divine side of regeneration, four agents are at work to bring a person to the new birth -

(1) We are born again *by the will of the Father* -

> *He gave us the right to become the children of God; because we are born, not by natural descent, nor by some human choice, nor by the decision of a spouse, but by an act of God* (Jn 1:12,13).

How this divine prerogative is exercised in relation to the new birth will be discussed later. The important thing to notice here is that the Father himself is the originator of the new birth. It is an expression of his own kindness and love.

Notice how scripture countermands the false notion some people have of a merci*ful* Jesus dying to placate a merci*less* God - as though all the initiative for our salvation stemmed from Christ, not from the Father. Yet the Bible says it was God who sent his only Son into the world to become the Saviour of the world (Jn 3:16). And Peter adds -

> *Blessed be the God and Father of our Lord Jesus Christ, for by his infinite mercy we have been born again to a living hope through the resurrection of Jesus Christ from the dead!* (1 Pe 1:3).

(2) We are born again *by the grace of the Son*, through our spiritual union with him -

> *Everyone who is in Christ has become a new creation; the old has passed away, and the new has come* (2 Co 5:17). Also, *God has given us eternal life, and this life is*

in his Son. If you have the Son then you have life; if you do not have the Son then you do not have life (1 Jn 5:11-12).

(3) We are born again ***by the action of the Holy Spirit***. It is the Spirit who brings into practical effect our union with Christ (Jn 3:5-6).

(4) We are born again *by the **word of God*** -

You have been born anew, not of perishable seed, but of imperishable, through the living and abiding word of God (1 Pe 1:23; see also He 4:12).

In those references, and others like them, two things appear -

first, the word of God itself has life; it is "living and active"; it possesses a creative dynamic, a power to destroy or to build (Je 23:29); it is inherently mighty and filled with energy. But

second, the word by itself cannot regenerate a human life. The Holy Spirit must take hold of that word and use it to bring conviction of sin and a revelation of Christ.

So then, the new birth results when the Holy Spirit energises the understanding of those who hear the word, so that they believe and receive the promise of life. Only then, when the word is mixed with faith in response to the Spirit, can it become an imperishable seed of life in the human soul. Out of that seed the regenerated soul is born.

THE HUMAN SIDE

On the human side of regeneration, we are born again by a three-fold response -

(1) By ***repentance***, which means a deep sorrow for sin, and a wholehearted turning away from sin -

Repent and abandon all your wrongdoing . . . Cast far away all the transgressions that you have committed against me, and embrace a new heart and a new spirit! Do you really want to die?... Yet I find no pleasure in the death of any one, says the Lord God. So turn back to me and live! (Ez 18:30-32; see also 2 Ch 7:14; Is 55:7; Ac 17:30; 2 Co 7:10).

(2) By <u>*receiving and believing*</u> in Christ (Jn 1:12-13).

(3) By <u>*believing the word of God*</u> -

God has put into our hands his precious and very great promises, so that through them you might become sharers in his own divine nature and escape the corruption that evil passions have brought into the world *(2 Pe 1:4; and 1 Jn 5:10-11)*.

Note: the word *"believe"* here means much more than mental assent to the truth. Rather, it adds to the idea of intellectual agreement the concept of *"fully rely upon"*, *"adhere to,"* *"fully committed to."*

The sense is not merely one of head-knowledge, but of heart-experience; not just a mental exercise, but a total life-commitment; an inner passion must be integrated with what is accepted as true. In other words, the Holy Spirit is looking for a *faith response* to the promises of God that will lead to a new life-style.

Saving faith therefore is an act of both heart and mind: with the *mind* the truth of the gospel is accepted; but out of the *heart* comes a dedication to live in accordance with the gospel. So belief is not satisfied by *passive* assent, but only the kind of *active* agreement that leads to personal involvement -

> *What profit can it bring you, my friends, if you say that you have faith but your actions do not match what you say? Can such a "faith" save you? ... So faith by itself, if it lacks corresponding action, is dead. ... For just as a body apart from its spirit is dead, so faith apart from proper actions is dead* (Ja 2:14,17-18,24-26).

Affirmation is also involved in saving faith, for it is the confession of our lips that seals the salvation of God in our lives (Lu 6:45; Mt 10:32-33; Ro 10:9-10) - but this is more fully discussed in my book, *Faith Dynamics*.

THE IMPERATIVE OF THE NEW BIRTH

To Nicodemus, the rich preacher who was yet unsaved, Jesus said, *"You must be born again!"* Then he told Nicodemus how to seize the new birth -

> *In the same way that Moses lifted up the brass snake in the wilderness, the Son of Man must be lifted up, so that whoever believes in him may have eternal life* (Jn 3:14-15).

Jesus was that Son of Man who was lifted up on the cross. His purpose was to die for the sins of the human race, so that we might believe in him and not perish in the judgment that must follow the grave.

Christ made this supreme sacrifice in obedience to the love of God -

> *For God so loved the world that he gave his only Son, so that whoever believes in him may not perish but receive eternal life* (vs. 16).

Still further, the Lord went on to say that he had not come into the world to destroy it, but to bring abundant life to all who are willing to receive it. He said,

> *For God did not send his Son into the world to condemn the world, but that the world might be saved through him (vs. 17).*

On the other hand, if any man or woman fails to believe in Christ, those people will have to face him when he returns to this earth in glory; and when he comes again it will be as Judge, not Saviour.

So with all solemnity the Master warned -

> *Anyone who believes in me will not be condemned; but anyone who does not believe is condemned already, because that person has not believed in the name of the only Son of God* (vs. 18).

You may be young in years, but it makes no difference, you *must* be born again. And if you are old, you can *still* be born again. The record of the past, the stain of the past, the domination of the past, can all be taken from you. Any human being can experience the regenerative power of the Holy Spirit, through Christ, and so enter a new dimension of life.

THE CERTAINTY OF THE NEW BIRTH

It is impossible for a person to be born again and not know it, for God puts within us a spiritual witness that we have become a new creation in Christ (see Ro 8:16; Ga 4:6; 1 Jn 5:10).

The life in any creature bears witness of itself, and needs no justification for its existence, nor any explanation. It is enough to live, and those who are alive know it! So is everyone who is truly born of the Spirit.

However, doubts may still arise within us about the veracity of this witness, or about the validity of our faith. We may be enticed to question whether or not God has accepted us into his family. Our sense of his divine life may fade or even vanish altogether. Hence the need to understand the theme of your next chapter - *justification by faith*.

CHAPTER TWO - PART ONE:

JUSTIFICATION

> The distinction between law and gospel is the highest art in Christendom, which should be grasped and understood by all who call themselves Christians. Where this is not done, a Christian cannot be distinguished from a heathen or a Jew. So much depends on this distinction! . . . In fact everything depends on the proper separation of these two messages . . . otherwise you will neither know nor retain a true understanding of one or the other; nay, while under the impression of having both, you will have neither. . . . Therefore whoever has mastered this ability to distinguish the law from the gospel, place him at the head of the list and call him a Doctor of Holy Scripture. For without the Holy Spirit, it is impossible to make this distinction [4]

Not everyone would agree with Luther that the distinction between law and grace is the central issue of the gospel; but all will allow that this distinction is a vital part of apostolic preaching, especially of Paul. Centuries before Luther was born, the great apostle to the gentiles asserted that a clear understanding of what it means to be *justified by faith* (apart from your own good works) is a vital key to steadfast, mature, and successful life in Christ.

But what *is* this difference between law and gospel? What does it mean to be *"justified by faith alone"*?

"Justification" is a *legal* term. It is used in the NT (especially by Paul) to present what is called a *forensic* explanation of the salvation the Father has given us in Christ. This is in contrast, say, to the *sacerdotal* (priestly)

---

[4] Martin Luther, in a New Year's sermon for 1532, on Ga 3:23-24.)

explanation given in the letter to the *Hebrews*; or to the *regenerative* explanation given in your previous chapter. [5]

In other words, the writer of *Hebrews* explains salvation as something achieved by a priestly sacrifice at God's altar, while John explains it in terms of a new birth; but Paul (when he uses the expression *"justification"*) thinks of salvation as an act of acquittal in a court of law, an acquittal that comes to us solely in response to faith in Christ [6] (see Ro 1:17; 3:28; 5:1; Ga 2:16; 3:11,24; He 10:38).

AN ACT OF ACQUITTAL

In all three languages, Hebrew, Greek, and English, a *"justified"* man is one who has stood in the dock for sentencing, but has been pronounced innocent, and therefore released from the charges that were laid against him.

Notice something *very* important: a legal sentence is not an act of power, but simply a verbal declaration. It has three vital limitations -

ACQUITTAL REQUIRES ONLY LEGAL INNOCENCE

You must have noticed how our law courts sometimes condemn innocent people and acquit guilty ones. That is because, in practice, the law does

---

[5] See again the preface and the second footnote of your previous chapter.

[6] As I have already indicated (see the Footnote immediately above), these ideas reflect various attempts to explain the inexplicable - the height, depth, and breadth of the amazing salvation God has given us in Christ. Neither justification, nor regeneration, nor propitiation, nor any other concept, can fully embrace the wonder of all that God has done for us. But they each explore a different facet of divine grace; they each expose another dimension of divine promise; they each present a new opportunity to appropriate by faith the divine gift. There is, of course, no conflict between these varying concepts - they are not contradictory but complementary.

Our task and joy in this chapter will be to explore the legal aspect of our salvation, to follow what is called the <u>forensic</u> argument, to understand what the Bible means when it says that we are *"justified by faith"* (Ha 2:4; Ro 1:17; 3:28; 5:1; Ga 2:16; 3:11,24; 5:1; He 10:38).

not deal with the *factual* guilt or innocence of an accused person, but rather seeks only to discover whether his innocence or guilt can be *judicially* established. "A criminal trial is not a tribunal for eliciting truth." [7] Law courts are in the end concerned only with law.

Thus acquittal in a court of law does not really depend upon the *actual* innocence of the person who is on trial, but rather upon the failure of the prosecutor to prove any case against that person. Consequently, the accused is pronounced l*egally* innocent, and is discharged from the court free, and without penalty. He may in fact be guilty. Indeed, the judge, the lawyers, the jury, the spectators, may all *know* that he is guilty; but if his guilt cannot be established by lawful means the judge has no choice but to declare him innocent and to dismiss the case.

In the same way, God knows (and you know) you are guilty of offending heaven's law. God makes no attempt to change that. Instead, he has found a way to declare you *legally* innocent in Christ. You *are* a sinner; nonetheless he justifies you in Christ.

So remember: your justification in no way depends upon you establishing any kind of past, present, or future innocence in the sight of God. You are innocent of all charges, and free of all penalty, simply on the basis of the sentence that has been passed in your favour in the court of heaven.

That leads on to the second vital limitation.

Your justification is -

NOT DEPENDENT UPON MORAL CHANGE

A sentence spoken by a judge has no power to effect any change in a person's *character*; it changes only his *legal standing* within the community. No moral work is done in him. He simply shifts in his relationship to the law from a state of suspicion to one of acquittal. Whereas he once stood accused, now he is reckoned innocent. But *morally* he is still the same person.

---

[7]   P. D. James, <u>Death of an Expert Witness</u> Book II, Sec. 3.

Likewise, our justification is an act of *declaration*, not an act of *power*. It is a work of God external to the sinner, not something accomplished within his nature. It has to do with a change in God's attitude toward us and a change in our relationship to his law. Whereas we once lay under the wrath of God, now, being justified, we are admitted to his favour, cleared of all the charges that were laid against us.

There are some who endeavour to attach a moral sense to justification. That is, they view it as arising from, or at least incorporating, an act of divine power within the believer's own life. They associate with justification a transforming work of grace that makes the believer holy.

Now in a little while I will be stating vigorously that true justification *should* lead on to a sanctified and obedient life. But that is a *fruit* of justification, not a basis for it, nor even an integral part of it.

So rid yourself of the idea that you cannot claim to be justified unless a moral change has happened in your behaviour. Especially, discard the notion that before you can declare yourself justified before God, you must effect a moral change in yourself by your own effort.

The constant meaning of *"justify"* (and other parallel words) in both Old and New Testaments, enforces the idea that it belongs without any moral sense in a strictly *forensic* setting. If justification contains anything more than a simple legal significance, then it differs in no material way from sanctification, and many biblical statements become meaningless.

This can be seen in the following -

(1) In many places a strictly forensic sense is the only possible meaning of *justify* - to give it a moral sense makes the statements ridiculous (see De 25:1; Pr 17:15; Is 5:23; 53:11; Ro 3:20; 4:5,8; Ga 3:11; 5:4).

(2) The word *"condemnation"* is often used in antithesis to justification; but since condemning a man does not in itself make him wicked, neither does justifying him in itself make him righteous. Both terms express only a person's state in the eyes of the law. In addition to some of the above references (see also Ro 8:33-34; Ge 18:25).

(3) Expressions equivalent to *"justification"* clearly carry only a legal sense (see Ge 15:6; Ps 32:1-2; Ro 4:6-7; 2 Co 5:19; Ja 2:23).

(4) A moving example of the transfer of guilt and of innocence from one to another is found in Philemon (see vs. 17-18). Onesimus had greatly wronged his master, Philemon. But Onesimus was Paul's friend. So the apostle asks that all of his own good qualities should be accepted as belonging to the slave. Philemon should receive Onesimus as he would do Paul himself. And, in turn, Paul offers to take all of the slave's guilt to himself, and to discharge any wrong that may have been done to Philemon. Paul's innocence was to be given to Onesimus, and the guilt of Onesimus was to be charged against Paul.

So, to justify a person means simply to set him again in a *right relationship* either to the law or to another person. For us, this means the law of God and God himself. In the case of a person who is actually free from guilt, justification involves simply a vindication of his innocence. But where there has been actual wrongdoing, as in our case, justification can be achieved only by some means that fully expiates that guilt. God has found that means in Christ.

Our position can therefore be summarised -

> Although we are guilty and deserve punishment, God, in
> a legal and just response to the atonement Christ has
> made, pardons us, clears us from all guilt, and accepts us
> as being actually righteous in the sight of his law.

Thus, though your guilt may be factually undeniable, your innocence is legally undeniable; God must therefore deal with you as though you had never sinned. Does that mean you should be content to remain guilty in fact and only innocent in law? Of course not! As I have said above, this change in *legal* relationship is emphatically intended by God to lead us on into a change of *life* relationship. Justification does not in itself cause any moral change or inner transformation, but it *does* pave the way for such a change to be wrought later by the Holy Spirit.

Thus the outward imputation of righteousness in *justification* becomes the basis for an inward infusion of holiness in *sanctification*.

Remember this: never base your claim of justification upon whether or not you have reformed morally. Your justification does not depend upon *any* internal change, whether wrought by you or by God. It is a wholly legal matter, based on the just acquittal God has secured for you in Christ.

That takes us on to the third vital limitation: your justification depends upon

A HEAVENLY WORD, NOT AN EARTHLY WORK

Here is the single greatest thing you can understand about justification: *it results from a word already spoken in heaven, not from an act being performed on earth.* The entire transaction is a heavenly not an earthly one, based solely upon the merits of Christ and his substitutionary death. Seeing the cross, and the victory over sin Christ gained there, the Father has spoken in heaven the sentence of acquittal for all who believe in Jesus.

If justification depended upon some ongoing work of mine on earth, then a thousand misadventures could undermine it. But happily, I know it is not my *work* but the Father's *word* that justifies. He has given me a verdict of acquittal entirely because of what Christ has done. The Cross is rooted in history, and cannot be changed; the justifying sentence is recorded in heaven, far beyond the interfering reach of men or demons. Upon those two unassailable guarantees I base my claim of innocence in Christ.

So you and I are left with no other choice except to believe or reject the word the Father has spoken. Upon that simple choice our eternal destiny hangs.

Does that mean there are *no* earthly ramifications to justification? Of course not. It is expected of any person who walks out of a courtroom as a free citizen that he will at once resume all the rights and benefits that are rightfully his. So should you do before God. Peace and joy, access to the throne of God, answered prayer, all of God's promises, are lawfully yours in Christ and cannot be lawfully denied to you. Have you heard the Judge pronounce that sweet word *"Justified"*? Then boldly claim all that belongs to you as a free-born citizen of the kingdom of God!

THE COMPONENTS OF JUSTIFICATION

PARDON

In this forensic understanding of justification there is one point at which the analogy breaks down. In the ordinary processes of a court of law, a man must first plead *"Not guilty!"* and then hope he will be acquitted on the basis of his legally proven innocence. Being shown to be legally guiltless, the accused person is set free.

But when an accused sinner stands before heaven's bar the position is altered. In that court all of us are indisputably guilty, and a plea of *"Not guilty!"* will not be accepted. So we have the remarkable scene of guilty persons coming before the tribunal, frankly acknowledging their guilt, knowing they deserve death, yet nonetheless walking out from the presence of the judge fully discharged from all charges and free from all penalty!

The Judge says *"Not guilty!"* only after we say *"Guilty!"* The death penalty is remitted only after we put our necks in the noose!

The key to this legal anomaly lies in the fact that we are able to claim as our own the innocence of another, our Saviour, the Lord Jesus Christ. That claim enables God to acquit us, because Christ has made available to us the full measure of his own righteousness (2 Pe 1:1). But never forget, that gift is available only to those who first acknowledge their guilt, and then flee to Christ for refuge. Hence the first word of the gospel is always, *"Repent!"* (Mt 4:17).

For that reason, into heaven's justification another element enters, namely, *pardon*.

On earth, pardon would be angrily rejected by one who had been proven innocent. But we have pleaded *"Guilty!"* and stand openly condemned before God; therefore Christ offered himself as our ransom so that God might pardon us, and along with that pardon also work the miracle of reckoning us to be fully innocent.

That is indeed a marvellous work of grace!

Pardon means remission of punishment, release from penalty; it has to do, not with the removing of sin itself, but with overlooking, or removing, the penalty for sin.

Because of our faith in the sacrifice of Christ, even though we are actually guilty, God treats us as though we are innocent. This incredible mercy is expressed in the following: *Micah 7:18-19; Isaiah 55:7; Psalm 78:38; 85:2-3; 2 Samuel 12:13; Romans 4:5.* Let your heart sing with gratitude as you read and trust those promises.

Notice that in each passage God *reckons* innocence upon his people (even though they are guilty), and on the basis of that reckoning turns aside the penalty that otherwise would have been theirs.

But that reckoning is possible only because our penalty has fallen upon Christ. By his death the demands of the law were satisfied, thus enabling God to free us from condemnation.

Clearly then, your justification rests on no personal merit, but wholly lies in that free act of God's love and grace whereby, for the sake of Christ and through your faith in him, God considers you guiltless, and brings you into the fulness of his grace.

FORGIVENESS

"Forgiveness" is more personal than *"pardon"*. It is not the word of a violated law, but rather of an offended friendship. Here is injured love refusing to hold to anger, but absolving the offender from all blame, and treating him as though the hurt had never been done.

In ordinary life one person may be compelled to pardon another - especially if in court no case can be proved against his foe - yet he may never yield his heart to forgiveness. Though legally he is unable to exact vengeance or recompense, he can still burn with anger against the offender, and he can forever exclude the debtor from his friendship and love.

God, however, has not only removed from us all legal *penalty*, he has also turned aside his *anger*. He asks for no reparation. He bears no ill will. He gladly welcomes into the fold of his love all who accept his free gift of salvation in Christ (see Ne 9:17; Ps 103:8-11; Ep 1:7).

PEACE

It is true that justification is primarily a legal declaration. Nonetheless, those who have received this acquittal, and who truly believe the promise of God, will surely feel some kind of inner response of joyous peace.

That inner response is not an essential part of justification itself, but rather a natural corollary of the justified state. If you truly *know* that you have been justified by faith in Christ, then you will find an immediate release from the guilt and bitterness of a sin-stricken conscience. That in turn leads to a sense of peace with God, and peace with oneself.

How the troubled heart of man longs for that double peace! What treasures people have expended in an effort to bring an end to warfare within their own flesh, and between themselves and God! Yet without price, without struggle, that longed-for cessation of hostilities comes upon every believer who awakens to the fact that he is no longer under sentence of death, and that all recollection of his guilt has been removed from heaven.

How could it be otherwise? It is futile to remain under a guilty oppression for crimes of which we are no longer considered guilty; in fact, for crimes we are now reputed never to have committed!

That justification involves forgiveness of sin is seen in *Isaiah 43:5; Acts 13:38-39*; and that this justification issues in peace, is seen in *Romans 5:1*.

But what if, after we are justified, we should again fall into sin?

The references quoted so far show that, so long as faith in Christ is maintained, *no guilt can be laid against us, no condemnation can be brought down upon us.* Can we then continue to sin with impunity? Will we suffer no injury? Will sin cause us no loss?

Hardly! It is true, when God justifies us he also removes all of the guilt of our sin. But the awful wickedness of sin itself remains. It is always a criminal act, a violation of God's law. Because of this, when we sin we are at once gripped by a sense of our culpability; we feel our fellowship with God has been broken; shame and remorse overwhelm us. Because of our faith in Christ, we do remain justified in the sight of God, but we cannot escape the deep loss and injury sin always causes. David expressed that pain in his sorrowful lament - see *Psalm 51:3,4,8,11,12.*

However, as David also shows, that very consciousness of loss is intended to drive us to repentance again, and to cause us once more to seek the comforting assurance that we are *"accepted in the Beloved."*

Some may say, however, that such a loss of peace and fellowship is a small price to pay for sin; they will gladly bear a little spiritual pain if they may live as they please. But against that folly the following objections rise up in anger -

First, sin is a dread poison; it is not only a crime against God but also against *ourselves*. It has in it the sting of death. It corrupts, poisons, and sears the conscience; it brings destruction into body, soul, and spirit.

People who sin wilfully, thinking they are safely hidden in the justification of Christ, soon find their sin decays their faith; they grieve the Holy Spirit who is their only seal until the day of redemption; they lose the capacity for repentance; they ultimately scorn and spurn Christ himself. Dreadful is the woe pronounced against them by scripture (see Ga 6:7-8; He 6:4-6; 10:26-31).

Second, how can a person who, by exercising faith in the divine promise of justification, has sought peace with God now deliberately and wilfully continue doing the very things which must destroy that peace? How can a person who has hungrily sought after righteousness, and has found it in Christ, suddenly make that discovery a ground upon which to live unrighteously?

In fact the very opposite is true. Being justified, the scripture says, a true believer's one desire is to make faith the ground of real holiness, so that, having found peace with God through Christ, he now presses on into increasing fellow ship with God, and into conformity with the Father's will (Ro 5:1-2).

RECONCILIATION

AN ACT OF RESTORED FELLOWSHIP

Justification must include reconciliation; if it were not so, we might find ourselves in the unhappy position of being only discharged criminals, still with immense difficulties to overcome, still with the dark and heavy load of our past crimes dogging our way. Pardon, and even forgiveness, do not in themselves mean restoration to a place of full trust. We might be released from our legal penalty, and we might be accepted as friends, and yet might still not be accepted as worthy of trust and responsibility.

Therefore God, when he justifies us, also *reconciles* us to himself. That means, not only does he see us as righteous at the present moment, but he considers us as having *always* been righteous.

This promise of reconciliation is seen in such statements as, *"he will remember our sins no more . . . he will cast all of our sins into the depths of the sea . . . he will remove our transgressions as far as the east is from the west. . . "* - and so on.

Now, if God *reckons* you to be innocent of all sin, then he will naturally *treat* you as someone innocent of all sin. That is, he will grant you access to all his favour. He will give you all that he would have given you had you in fact *not* fallen. He will, in a word, show you the same kind of benevolence as he did to Jesus!

But remember, we are justified only as we stand in Christ, united to Christ by faith. We are accepted only *"in the Beloved"*. But if we do stand firm in Christ, refusing to be moved away from him by anything, not even by sin, then all of the favour that belongs to Christ God will freely bestow on us (Cl 1:22; Ro 8:16-17a; 5:1-2; 2 Co 5:21).

So then, if you are *justified*, you may also accept that you are *reconciled*: that is, mutual trust and confidence are restored between you and God. Once you were estranged, but now there is perfect accord. The things that hindered your approach to God and his approach to you have been removed; the thoughts and the ways that placed you at variance with the Lord have been nailed to the cross; harmony reigns in place of discord, friendship in place of antagonism, favour in place of indignation.

AN ACT OF REMOVED ENMITY

Another aspect of reconciliation must be considered. Does it describe offending man's reconciliation with an angry God, or a loving God's reconciliation with hateful man? Am I taking steps to regain God's friendship, or is he taking steps to regain mine? Or is the process reciprocal?

James Stewart prepares the way for such questions by writing:

> Reconciliation means the establishing of friendly relations between parties engaged in a quarrel. Now clearly there are more ways than one in which such a peace-making may happen. Much depends on the nature of the estrangement. If the resentment has been mutual, then fellowship can be re- established only when both parties agree to put their angry feelings away. If the enmity has been on one side, harmony may be restored

> either by a deliberate change of feeling in the hostile mind, or by a friendly approach from the other side which disarms antagonism. [8]

How do those ideas apply to us? Stewart continues -

> (Other religions) take it for granted that God is the one who needs to be reconciled. Ritual acts and offerings are prescribed through which the offended deity may be placated.

That idea is not absent from Christianity, but the main focus of the gospel is on the reverse: *that man is the enemy who must be reconciled to God.* Stewart, in fact, argues that this is the only view of reconciliation presented in the NT. That position seems rather extreme (as I shall show in a moment), but it cannot be denied that the overwhelming emphasis in the NT is that Christ has reconciled man to God, not God to man. So Stewart writes -

> With one voice the pagan creeds declare that man must take steps to reconcile his God, and so restore himself to favour. Christianity cuts clean across this, and declares the exact opposite. God is the Reconciler. God, in his changeless and unwearying love, has taken the initiative, has broken into the atmosphere of man's hostility, and has thrown down every estranging barrier that guilt and hopelessness and dull resentment can erect . . . it is God who reconciles, man who is reconciled. [9]

That is certainly the sense of the following references. In the first of them notice that the act of reconciliation is directed toward us, not God -

> *While we were enemies, we were reconciled to God by the death of his Son* (Ro 5:10).

Notice in the next reference, it is *man* who is called upon to cease hostilities, and to accept the divine proffer of friendship -

---

[8] A Man In Christ, Hodder & Stoughton, London, 1972, pg. 209.
[9] Ibid. pg. 211.

> *God through Christ reconciles us to himself . . . God was in Christ reconciling the world to himself, not reckoning their wrongdoing against them . . . We plead with you on behalf of Christ, be reconciled to God* (2 Co 5:18-20). And again: *Once you were cut off from God, full of anger against him, always committing sin; but now he has reconciled you through the death of Christ so that he may present you to himself holy, blameless, and faultless* (Cl 1:21-22).

It is important to emphasise this Christian view of reconciliation, because too many people hold to the idea that God sits in heaven implacably angry, scarcely restrained from destroying humanity even by the pleas of Christ. There is an idea that God is all law while Christ is all love, that all the initiative for our salvation comes from Christ, while God acts only in judgment. But that is absurd. As I mentioned in your last chapter, it was *"<u>God</u> (who) so loved the world that he gave his only Son, that whoever believes in him should not perish but have eternal life"* (Jn 3:16).

Man was implacable, not God. The barriers were erected on earth, not in heaven. However, it required an act of God to remove those barriers and to provide a way for man to shake off his antagonism and to return to the Father's family.

But having said that, it must still be admitted that Christ's reconciling work is not concerned only with man. There is certainly some sense in which heaven's offended righteousness also had to be placated. On this, Leon Morris writes -

> That which set up the barrier was the demand of God's holiness for uprightness in man. Man, left to himself, is content to let bygones be bygones. He is not particularly worried by his sin. Certainly he feels no hostility to God on account of his sin. The barrier arises because God demands holiness in man. Therefore when the process of reconciliation has been affected, it is impossible to say it is completely man-ward and not God-ward in any sense. There must be a change from God's side if all that is

involved in such expressions as "the wrath of God" is no longer to be (directed against) man. [10]

ADOPTION

To those who have found peace with God, and reconciliation, through Christ, there comes a further gift: membership in the family of God. Paul speaks of this progression:

> *In Christ Jesus you who were once far off have now been brought near through the blood of Christ. <u>For he is our peace</u>, now that he has broken down the wall of hostility that stood between us. His purpose was to <u>reconcile us to God</u>. through the cross, thereby bringing all enmity to an end. So then, you are no longer strangers but you are fellow citizens with the saints and <u>members of the family of God</u>* (Ep 2:13-19).

Clearly, peace and reconciliation lead on to a new family relationship with God. This is called *adoption*.

Once again we are faced with a *legal* expression, and with an act that affects our outward relationship with God, but not necessarily our inward life.

Now if you realise you are an adopted child of God, and you can share in all of the good things belonging to his family, you will surely feel great joy and satisfaction. And this in turn will give you a desire to honour the Father in the highest way. But those are natural responses to adoption, not an integral part of it.

The position may become clearer if I make a careful distinction between the two expressions used in scripture to describe our family relationship with God.

Depending on the truth that is being expressed, the Bible sometimes describes us as the *adopted* children of God, and sometimes as the spiritually *reborn* children of God.

---

[10] <u>New Bible</u> Dictionary, Intervarsity Fellowship, London article, "Reconciliation", pg. 1077, edition 1967.

The first expression refers to a *legal* act by which we are brought into the Father's family, given his name, and become his heirs; but no inward change is necessarily implied - any more than there is in ordinary life when a child is adopted.

The second expression refers to a *spiritual* act by which we are brought to a moral rebirth, an inner renewal, the mystery of regeneration. This event takes place in all who truly confess Christ as Saviour; we are *"born again"*, and become the supernaturally created children of God.

Or, we could say that *adoption* has to do with the legal activity of justification; but *regeneration* has to do with the moral activity of sanctification. The first concerns God as King and Judge. The second concerns him as Creator and Father. The one expresses our outer relationship with God; and the other refers to our inner relationship. The one shows a change in legal status and condition; the other shows a change in life experience and character.

Those two aspects are often found side by side -

> *You are no longer controlled by your sinful nature but by the Spirit, providing the Spirit of God really lives in you. Anyone who does not have the Spirit of Christ does not belong to Christ* (Ro 8:9).

That is regeneration; but Paul then adds,

> *you have received the spirit of adoption* (Ro 8:15).

Again we find the legal aspect -

> *God sent his Son to redeem those who were under the law, so that we might be adopted as his sons* (Ga 4:4-5).

Which Paul follows by stressing the practical and personal outcome of that adoption:

> *And because you are his (adopted) children, God has sent the Spirit of his Son into our hearts, crying, "Abba! Father!"* (Ga 4:6).

There are three more comments to make on our adoption -

(1) Some writers, trying to arrive at firm definitions, argue that adoption is the first and essential step in the process that brings us eventually into true sonship. Others reverse that idea, and argue that the new

birth is the sole ground of our adoption and that *"adoption"* is used in the NT to describe our attainment of the status of adult sons. Both views seem to be unnecessarily rigid. A survey of the NT indicates that the apostles were by no means so fine in their use of these words.

It is better to say that the work of adoption and the work of the new birth go hand in hand, they both spring into being the moment we put our faith in Christ - they simply express different aspects of the things God has wrought for us in Christ.

And while, on the one hand, the basic aspects of both adoption and sonship are completed the moment we yield our lives to Christ, on the other hand there are dimensions in each relationship that we are still entering into, including some that we will not experience until Christ returns (Ro 8:23; Ep 4:13).

> (2) Again, in the act of adoption, we find a work that springs solely from the grace of God. There is nothing we have done in the past that could merit our welcome into God's family, and there is nothing we can do now to merit remaining there. Of his own free and boundless love the Father has adopted us in Christ -
>
> > *He predestinated us in love to be his adopted sons through Jesus Christ* (Ep 1:5).

The prophet saw this marvellous thing happening -

> *For you alone are our Father, though Abraham does not know us and Israel does not acknowledge us. Yet you, O Lord, remain our Father, and your name from long ago is still Redeemer* (Is 63:16).

This adoption, in all of its potential, is fully and freely given to you immediately on your confession of faith in Christ -

> *For in Christ Jesus you are all children of God through faith* (Ga 3:26).

> (3) This gracious adoption opens to us a number of rich and wonderful privileges, such as
>
> > ➢ prayer, no longer the begging of an estranged pauper, but rather a child's confident request to its Father (Ro 8:15-16).

- ➢ the special love and favour no stranger can know, but that the Father delights to show to his own children (Ep 5:1; 1 Jn 3:1).
- ➢ removal forever of the isolation, fear, and trembling of a slave (Ga 4:4-7).
- ➢ no longer condemned or treated like sinners, but dealt with as children, in love, and for the purpose of making us righteous (He 12:5-11). We can still be punished - but only as children, by our Father; we cannot be penalised as criminals, by the Judge!
- ➢ the Father's provision and protection (Mt 6:31-32; 10:29-31).
- ➢ a glorious brotherhood with Christ and with the other members of the divine family (Ep 2:19; He 2:11).
- ➢ an eternal and equal inheritance with Christ (Ro 8:17).

As if the above were not riches enough, God by his grace has also given to adoption future use: it describes the resurrection of the body at the coming of Christ. At that time we shall finally enter into all that membership in God's family means (Ro 8:18-23; 1 Jn 3:2; Lu 20:36; 1 Pe 1:3-5).

(Continued in the next chapter.)

42

CHAPTER TWO - PART TWO:

JUSTIFICATION

This chapter continues the theme of *justification*, that great word of divine acquittal spoken on behalf of those who believe in Jesus.

The heading numbers follow on from your previous chapter.

We have seen what the word means, and what benefits are given to us along with our justification in Christ. Now we answer the question of how God is able to acquit the unjust and to pronounce them righteous -

THE BASIS OF JUSTIFICATION

THE LOVE OF GOD

> See Jeremiah 31:3; Romans 3:24; John 3:16; Ephesians 2:4-5; 1 John 3:1; etc.

Love is the impulse that moved the heart of God to provide a way of escape for us; but God's *love* had to accord with God's *justice*. Hence there was need for a proper ground on which the call of the love of God for mercy could be satisfied, without contradicting the call of the law of God for justice. The ground provided by God was the obedience of the Lord Jesus Christ. Because he died we live; because he obeyed we are rewarded. Through Christ *"all things are ours, and we are Christ's, and Christ is God's"* (1 Co 3:21-23). So the second basis upon which our justification stands is -

THE OBEDIENCE OF CHRIST

You must resolutely banish from your mind all thought of securing justification, or any part of justification, by any work of your own.

If you and I are to be justified at all in the sight of God, it must be solely upon the merits of Christ -

HUMAN MERIT CANNOT JUSTIFY

It is essential to abandon ruthlessly all thought of earning access to God by collecting together a package of noble works (Tit 3:5; Ro 4:24b-5:2, 8-11).

It is quite foolish to rest on your own goodness as the key to acceptance by the Father. Even at its very best, your goodness remains imperfect, tainted with sin.

> It is impossible for you or me to find any kind of acquittal from guilt by any thing we can do of ourselves. *"All have sinned and come short of the glory of God,"* and we can regain that glory only when we are *"justified by God's grace as a gift through the redemption that is in Christ Jesus" (Ro 3:23-24).*

Even if you are not conscious of any sin in your life you still dare not claim any personal merit as a basis for gaining the favour of God (1 Co 4:4).

JUSTIFICATION LEADS TO SANCTIFICATION

Many people are trying to work up some kind of holiness, which they hope will then qualify them to lay hold of God's promise of justification.

But that attitude ignores what we have already seen: *justification causes no direct change in moral character.* It merely brings the believer into a changed relationship with God. From being his enemy we become his friend. But that changed relationship then becomes the ground on which God is able to send the Spirit of sanctification into our lives.

You must grip this fact!

There are so many who fail to enter into the joy and peace of justification because they are still aware of sin in their lives. Until they are free of *sin* they feel that they dare not call themselves *innocent*!

But sin cannot *be* overcome until we first grasp the fact that it is all forgiven, that we are absolutely free from condemnation, that we are wholly restored to the favour of God, and thus are able to approach the throne of God boldly. There is no way to shake loose from the *power* of sin until we are first freed from its *guilt*. How can it be otherwise? Your own hand will never pry you out of sin's grip.

Only the hand of God has enough strength. But you cannot get near God, to find his help, while sin's stench is still upon you. You *must* run first to the Cross, and be washed in the blood of the Lamb, before you can walk to the Throne and find grace to help you in your time of need! (He 10:17-22; 4:16).

The beginning of all victory over sin lies in a bold appropriation by faith of the perfect justification God has given us in Christ - and you cannot allow this appropriation either to be *encouraged* by your personal successes, nor *discouraged* by your personal failures. You are justified in *Christ*, absolutely independently of *anything* you are, or are not, in yourself.

The grace is his and the glory is his!

It is enough for us humbly to receive God's free gift.

Stand then, with simple trust in God's free gift, upon the ground of your full justification in Christ. That alone is the basis upon which you can press into ever increasing conformity to his divine nature. But this *"conforming"*, this *"growing in grace"*, this rising from *"glory to glory"*, this *"pressing on"*, is sanctification, and sanctification will never lead to, but always stems from, justification.

THE WORK OF CHRIST IN JUSTIFICATION

CHRIST FULFILLED THE PRECEPTS OF THE LAW

In the thirty three years of his life on earth the Lord Jesus Christ perfectly fulfilled every *precept* of the law of God, and by this complete obedience he has made available to us all of the *promises* of that law (Mt 5:19; He 5:8-9; 10:9-10).

CHRIST FULFILLED THE PENALTY OF THE LAW

In his death on the cross Christ totally exhausted the *penalty* of the law, and so wrought for us a complete *pardon* (Ro 5:9. etc.)

ONLY CHRIST COULD FULFILL BOTH PRECEPT AND PENALTY

If God could blot out all the record of your past failure, and then cause you to keep the law perfectly from that day on, it would still be insufficient, for the unfulfilled *penalties* of the law would continue to cry out for satisfaction.

But what if God were to condemn us all to bear the whole brunt of the law's fury, and to suffer all its penalties? That also would be insufficient, for then the *precepts* of the law would continue to yearn for fulfilment.

So the great question arose: how can both the precepts and the penalties of the law find satisfaction? *Christ was the answer.* He embraced both in himself. He satisfied the law's *precepts* by keeping them fully; he satisfied the law's *penalties* by enduring them at Calvary.

Had we been left to handle the problem by ourselves it would have remained impossible for us either to keep the precept or escape the penalty. Hence we are told: we could not talk our way out of judgment (Jb 11:2); sin has tainted the whole world and we cannot escape it (Jb 25:4-6); Satan has stricken us down, and only by the strength of God can we rise again (Ps 143:1-3); money cannot ransom us (Ps 49:7); we utterly deceive ourselves if we attempt to pronounce ourselves righteous (Jb 9:19-20).

So justification became ours solely by the free gift of God through the merits of Christ (Ro 5:16-19; 8:33; 10:3; Ph 3:9; Is 43:25-26; 53:11; etc.)

THE RESURRECTION OF CHRIST SEALED THE WORK OF GOD

The life and death of Christ fulfilled the demands of heaven for expiation of the broken law; but that alone could not have brought us any help. For another law, the law of death, was already at work in us. While Jesus' life and death satisfied the universal demand for righteousness, the need of individual men and women could be met only if the death that was already in them was replaced by life.

That great work was wrought for us when Christ conquered death on that first Easter morning (Ro 4:25; 8:2). Thus a magnificent double victory was gained over a dreadful double curse. Being justified by faith in Christ, we can now face both life and death with abounding joy!

THE INSTRUMENTAL MEANS OF JUSTIFICATION

FAITH IS THE SOLE INSTRUMENT

DEFINITION OF FAITH

There are various ways of defining *"faith"*; such as

- wholehearted acceptance of what scripture says about man's relationship with God;
- cheerful assent to the commands of scripture;
- total commitment of your life and will into the keeping of God;
- sincere trust in the unfailing goodness of God;
- and the like.

All those expressions of faith have a common quality: they are based upon the integrity and authority of the Word of God alone, without relying on any outside support. God has spoken in scripture, and faith needs no other buttress or nourishment. And nowhere is that more true than in the matter of justifying faith, which absolutely depends upon the testimony God has given us of his Son (1 Jn 5:9-12). When its goal is justification, faith takes the special form of absolute dependence upon the merits of Christ, followed by an unreserved surrender to the will of God.

Faith is an aggressive, active word. It does not describe merely a passive acceptance, a kind of quiescent belief, but rather exists in a setting of vigorous, joyful commitment of the whole life to Christ as Lord and Saviour.

Standing between the righteous and the wicked are two contrasting characteristics - not goodness and badness, because many of the wicked do things that are good, and the righteous often do things that are bad - rather, the distinguishing traits are self-sufficiency in the one, and God-sufficiency (or faith) in the other.

Faith then, is the singular factor in the life of a righteous man.

Faith will ultimately determine the believer's character and conduct.

Faith is the fundamental fact of Christian experience, it is the beginning of all real achievement for God.

THE NATURE AND VALUE OF FAITH

Having defined faith, we now need to limit it. Not limit its achievements, because faith brings us into vital union with the unlimited resources of God. But we do need to limit our concept of the place faith should occupy in our fellowship with God.

There are many who think that faith gives them virtue in the sight of God as though faith is a good work that conveys personal merit. But that would make justification stem from human effort, which is flatly denied by the scripture.

While the Bible does say that we are justified *"by"* or *"through"* faith, nowhere does it say that we are justified *on account of* faith. Justification is ours on account of *Christ*; faith is merely the instrument by which we appropriate that justification.

Faith then, is not a virtue that gives us credit with God, it is only part of the processes of divine law that enable us to be justified in Christ -

> *God justifies everyone who believes in Jesus. What then is left of our boasting? It is thrown out. On what principle? On the principle of keeping the law? No! It is on <u>the principle of faith!</u>* (Ro 3:26-27).

That we can claim no personal merit from our faith is further demonstrated by the fact that faith is as much the instrument of God as it is ours. It is *our* instrument, for *"a man is justified by faith"* (Ro 3:28); but it is also *God's* instrument, for *"it is God who will justify by faith . . . and through faith"* (vs. 30).

We are also told that such faith as we do have does not spring from ourselves, but is itself the gift of God (Ep 2:8; 6:23; Ro 12:3b,6).

Faith does not spring from our own strength or virtue, but from the sovereign grace of God (2 Th 2:13); it stems from Jesus Christ who is the universal Author of faith (He 12:2; Ac 3:16); it arises from the influence of the Holy Spirit (Ga 5:22b); it comes by means of hearing the Word of God (Ro 10:17; Ga 3:2,5).

Those sources are all outside of our personal achievement and come to us by the mercy of God alone. Hence we can claim no credit or merit in our faith, neither in its origin nor in its exercise.

Faith is therefore not the purchase price of salvation, it is only the *legal principle* that brings salvation to us; it is the means by which we accept an absolutely free gift of righteousness from Christ. We are saved *"by faith"* only in the sense that faith links us to Christ, who alone is the Saviour.

If faith itself were the basis of our justification, then we would observe varying degrees of salvation - for some are strong in faith whereas others are timid. We would also, as faith slowly strengthened, experience different levels of justification. But the fact is, trembling faith justifies as fully as bold faith. The bold may have a greater assurance of salvation, they may feel more strongly the joy and peace that belong to the children of God, but they do not receive any greater measure of the gift of God. The timid are as truly forgiven as the strong. God fully justifies all who believe in Jesus. Our justification is secured in heaven; it does not depend on earthly achievement.

Again, if faith were the ground of our salvation, and not solely the righteousness of Christ, then we would never be sure of eternal life, but would be left in anxious uncertainty. Why? Because faith is never perfect in this life, not even in the strongest among us. But thank God, he has excluded ALL human merit, and he has made the way to eternal life so simple and certain that the prophet could sing:

> *A highway shall be there, and it shall be called the Holy Way. God himself will walk there with you; not even the most foolish person can miss the way!* (Is 35:8, paraphrase).

FAITH IS THE UNCHANGING METHOD OF GOD

There is a tendency to think that God used to accept people on the basis of their obedience, therefore he will do so again. But the fact is, no-one has ever been accepted by the Lord who did not come to him in *faith*. Obedience has never been enough to give any man credit in the eyes of God. There is no merit, nor ever has been, in any work of yours or mine (Lu 17:10).

From the time of man's first transgression, only those who trusted solely in the righteousness that came down from heaven, and never in their own righteousness, have had access to God. The Bible shows no difference between the saving-faith of the old covenant and the saving-faith of the new covenant.

Although the terms *"faith"* and *"believe"* do not occur very frequently in the OT, it is nonetheless plain that the same cardinal law reigned then as it does now: *"the just shall live by FAITH"* (Ha 2:4; Ro 1:17; Ga 3:11; He 10:38; and cp. Jn 5:46; 12:38; Ro 10:16; 1 Pe 2:6).

From the earliest records of Genesis to the climax of the NT it is apparent that every saint of God has been characterised above all by *faith*.

The stories of Abel, Noah, Abraham, Moses, Joshua, etc., are all written to exhibit their walk of faith. Faith with them did not take the place of obedience, nor was faith a work of righteousness that secured them merit before God. On the contrary it was expected that obedience would issue *from* their faith, and their faith was proved by testing their obedience.

The patriarchs had faith; they lived obediently; yet many faults are recorded against their lives. How then were they justified? Solely by the gracious promise of God, and through their trust in that promise (see *Hebrews 11*).

And what was true of the patriarchs individually was evidently true of Israel as a whole. That is seen from many expressions in the OT which show clearly that the godly knew none of the legal observances could save them, and that the Lord alone, in whom they trusted, was the true *"hope of Israel"*. Thus we discover numerous phrases that express the life of faith: trusting in God; trusting in his Word, his name, his mercy, his salvation; finding refuge in God, or in the shadow of his wings; committing oneself to God, placing confidence in him, looking to him, relying on him, staying upon him, setting the heart upon him, binding to him in love, cleaving to him, hoping in God, waiting on him, etc.

So faith was the fundamental religious fact of the OT, just as it is in the NT. It was recorded in the days of the old economy, just as it now is under the gospel, that righteousness must come as a gift from the Lord God alone, or it will not come at all. Thus we read that

- ➢ salvation is a work of his free grace, it cannot be earned, it can only be gratefully received by faith (De 7:7; 8:18; 9:5; Am 3:2; Ho 13:5);
- ➢ pardon and restoration to fellowship come to those who depend for deliverance only upon God's mercy (Is 31:1; 57:13; Je 17:5; Ps 118:8; Jb 22:23-24);
- ➢ escape from sin's estranging guilt, and from judgment, belongs only to those who resolve to love God and to put their entire trust in him (Ps 63:1-3; 62:1-2; 86:1-3; 107:1-2);

- ➢ God accepted the sacrifices made on the altars of Israel only when the people looked beyond the altar and the plunging knife, and thrust their faith into the promise of God (Pr 15:8; Is 1:10-20; 66:1-4; Ho 6:6-7; Mi 6:6-8).

CHRIST - THE TRUE OBJECT OF FAITH

We often speak of believing the promise of God, of placing all our trust in his word. That is a proper thing to do, for God has given to his word a place of immense importance (Ps 138:2).

Nonetheless, the value of a promise depends wholly upon the nature of the one who promises. If you believe a promise, it is because you first believe the promiser.

Thus it is fine to believe the promise of God, so long as we look beyond that promise to God the promiser. We need a personal knowledge of God the Word as well as knowledge of the Word of God. Faith in the *promise* of God can only be as strong as our faith in *God* (see He 6:13-18).

Hence true saving faith is not primarily directed toward the promises that declare God's willingness to save, nor toward the actual work of salvation, *but rather toward the Saviour* who makes both the promise and the work effectual. It is not faith that saves us, but faith in the Lord Jesus Christ. It is not, strictly speaking, even faith in Christ that saves, but *Christ who saves through faith*.

Therefore, we are justified by faith only in the sense that faith brings us into union with Christ who is the Justifier. This union with Christ justifies us, not by an infusion of actual righteousness, nor by an impartation of the nature of Christ, *but simply by making it possible for God to impute to us the obedience of Christ*.

Further, even that union with Christ (insofar as it concerns justification) is not a combining union, nor a union of experience, it is only the union of *adoption*, whereby we are legally brought into the family of God.

Actually, the Bible describes a twofold union we have with Christ: in the first it is said that *"we are in Christ"*; in the second it is said that *"Christ is in us"*. The first applies to *justification*; the second applies to *regeneration*. The first is a work of legal *imputation*, external to the believer; the second is a work of life *impartation*, internal within the believer. Notice, however, the first is the ground of the second and necessarily precedes it.

Beware, though, of thinking that justification and regeneration can exist apart from each other. On the contrary, one without the other is equally impossible. If we are *"in Christ"* it is only that Christ might be *"in us"*. Hence, the *legal* work of *"adoption"*, which justifies us, is always associated with the *moral* work of regeneration, which makes us true *"born"* sons of God, and leads on to sanctification.

It would not be just for God to *pronounce* righteousness upon us without also *planting* in us a seed of holiness that would *produce* true righteousness in our conduct. But neither would it be possible for God to sow holiness in us without first removing the barrier of our past sin. Hence we see an unbreakable bond between justification and regeneration. Full salvation can be ours only as our faith in Christ leads both to our union with him and his union with us.

Some writers argue that the central truth of the gospel lies in the fact of our union with Christ. To them the greatest idea in the NT is not regeneration, nor justification, nor redemption, nor reconciliation, nor any other word, but rather the simple phrase *"in Christ!"* Here is an example -

> The heart of Paul's religion is union with Christ. This, more than any other conception - more than justification, more than sanctification, more even than reconciliation - is the key which unlocks the secrets of his soul. . . . Everything that religion meant for Paul is focused for us in such great words as these: *"I live, yet not I, but Christ liveth in me." "There is therefore now no condemnation to them which are in Christ Jesus." "He that is joined unto the Lord is one spirit."* . . . (If union with Christ is not kept central, then) the redemption achieved by Christ becomes something that operates mechanically or almost magically: it is altogether outside of us, independent of our attitude. Gore was not speaking too strongly when he declared that the tendency to isolate the thought "Christ for us" from the other thought "Christ in us" has been historically "an abundant source of scandal." . . . It is certain that such an idea as justification, for instance, can

only be gravely misleading when it is not seen in the light of a union with Christ in which the sinner identifies himself with Christ in his attitude to sin. [11]

HOW FAITH APPROPRIATES CHRIST
BY REPENTANCE

The first word in the gospel has always been, not *believe*, but *repent* (Mt 4:17). Faith must take its first step here, and here is where our justification begins. Christ declared that the *sorrowing* tax collector *"went down to his house justified"* - but the *satisfied* pharisee was rejected by God (Lu 18:14).

BY CALLING ON THE NAME OF JESUS

> *"You were justified in the name of the Lord Jesus Christ" (1 Co 6:11)*, which means acknowledging that his name, through faith in his name, opens to us all of the resources of heaven (Ac 3:16).

BY ACCEPTING THE EFFICACY OF THE BLOOD

> *See* Romans 3:24-26. *Concerning that vital passage note -*

(a) Justification begins with the grace of God; which means God treats us as having nothing, either good *or* bad, that can affect our position before him. He ignores both our goodness and our badness, and simply presents to those who believe his free gift of salvation.

"Grace" in connection with justification does not mean that God is willing to condone sin and to give salvation apart from any satisfaction of his offended law. It means rather the method whereby the love of God

---

[11] James Stewart, op. cit. pg. 147, 152. Perhaps Dr. Stewart has pushed the pendulum too far to the other side; but his emphasis is needed in some quarters. The real point, though, is not whether "justification by faith" is a more important idea than "union with Christ", or vice versa, but simply that both ideas must be held together. They are two sides of the one coin. Neither can stand without the other.

has made it possible for the law to be fulfilled, for our crimes to be pardoned, and for eternal life to become ours.

We are justified *"freely"* or, for *"nothing"*; that is, without any price to pay on our part. Only man's twisted ego makes him think that his righteousness must precede God's grace. After all, grace and righteousness are both moral issues - who is to say which must come first, or which has greater value?

Man says his righteousness has more value and it puts God in his debt. But that pride is like a discarded *"menstrual rag"* to the Lord! Rather, heaven has decreed that the grace of God holds primacy, and that we must come to him apart from our own works, and humbly, by faith, receive his free gift.

> *(b)* This justification is made possible by the *"redemption"* that is *"in"* Christ Jesus. When we are united with Christ by faith, the price he paid on the cross is credited to us, and we are redeemed from all of the thraldom of guilt and death.
>
> *(c)* In particular, the faith that puts us *"in Christ"* and makes available to us his redemption, is *"faith in his blood"*. That does not mean crediting the blood with some magical power of its own. *"Faith in the blood"* means only faith in what the shed blood of Christ signifies. The blood has a divine testimony: *"it speaks better things than the blood of Abel"* (He 12:24). Abel's blood cried out from the ground for vengeance, but the blood of Jesus, sprinkled on the mercy seat before the Father in heaven (that is the significance of *"propitiation"*) pleads only for pardon.
>
> *(d)* Thus the perfect righteousness of God is revealed, and we see why he has shown forbearance for all the sins of the past. He has restrained his hand from judgment, knowing that the time would come when perfect atonement for all wrong would be wrought by Christ. Now that Christ has died, God is seen to be just, and also to be the justifier of those who believe in Jesus.

BY A SPOKEN CONFESSION OF FAITH

> *See Matthew 12:37; Romans 10:9-10; and cp. also Hebrews 10:19-23; 3:1.*

FAITH, LIFE, AND GOOD WORKS

Faith, in the biblical sense, is more than mere mental acceptance, or even heart perception of revealed truth. True faith requires an *inner assurance* of truth linked with definite commitment to an *outward course* of action (see Ja 2:19-20).

Real faith, in the Bible sense, changes the direction of life, it embraces every part of the being, it transforms one's whole outlook and behaviour.

On the other hand, and exactly opposed to faith, is unbelief. Unbelief may be expressed negatively as simply ignorance, or failure to understand. But the Bible concept of unbelief, as of faith, goes beyond this passive idea. It gives the much stronger description of unbelief as being actual rebellion.

Just as faith shows itself in active obedience, so unbelief shows itself in active disobedience, and thus leads to the wrath of God (see Jn 3:36; Ac 19:9; Ro 11:20; He 3:12,18-19).

The Bible treats unbelief, not as springing from ignorance alone (ignorance leads rather to a neutral *"non-belief"*), but as coming from a heart that is fundamentally antagonistic to God. Were men truly sincere, once the offer of salvation had been presented to them, they would leap to receive the gospel. But instead, their hearts are incorrigibly wicked, and they are filled with unbelief only because they stubbornly refuse to receive the truth (2 Th 2:10-12; see also Jn 3:19; 8:47).

The ungodly man is governed by his unbelief; he has surrendered to its dictates, it moulds his character, fills his being, drives him to damnation.

Conversely, the godly should be possessed by their faith; every moment of every day they should live by it; it should be to them infinitely more potent and real than was their former unbelief; it should compel them to press on toward the prize of God!

So the principle is clearly established: the faith that justifies will also, and inevitably, lead on to a faith that sanctifies; faith that brings God's imputation of righteousness must also bring God's impartation of holiness (see Ga 2:16-20).

THE HOLY SPIRIT AND JUSTIFICATION

If, as I said earlier, justification is essentially a word spoken in heaven, and not a work done on earth, does that mean the Holy Spirit has no part to play in your justification?

Not at all, for it is the specific task of the Holy Spirit to *"reprove the world of sin, and of righteousness, and of judgment"* (Jn 16:7-11). Hence, apart from the ministry of the Spirit not one of us would be justified, for only as we are brought under conviction of sin by the Holy Spirit do we realise our condemnation in the sight of God; and only as the Holy Spirit reveals the scripture to us (vs. 13-14) do we understand that our judgment has fallen on Christ and that we must flee to him for his free gift of righteousness (see 1 Co 6:11.)

Furthermore, by the ministry of the Holy Spirit we have proof that Christ is actually interceding for us in heaven, that he is truly risen from the dead, and that his sacrifice is fully accepted by the Father as atonement for our sins. Without this witness of the Holy Spirit we would have no definite proof of these things. We are told that we have an *"advocate"* in *heaven* (1 Jn 2:1); but we know this only because we also have an *"advocate"* on *earth* (Jn 14:16-17, 20). (In those verses, the word for *"advocate"* and *"comforter"* is the same in the Greek, viz. *"paraclete."*)

Hence we are told that there are three witnesses in heaven, the Father, the Word, and the Holy Spirit; and there are also three witnesses on earth, the Spirit, the water, and the blood (1 Jn 5:7-8,10a). The *heavenly* witnesses speak to the offended law of God, demonstrating that full atonement has been made for our sins, and that it is now proper for us to be admitted to citizenship in God's eternal king dom. The *earthly* witnesses speak to us in our fallen state, and assure us that the way is open for us to be reconciled to God, and to live as kings and priests before him (1 Pe 2:9-10).

Further, it will be noted that the Holy Spirit is a witness both in heaven and on earth, so that those who accept his testimony have a double confirmation given to them of the truth of their salvation.

THE TIME OF JUSTIFICATION

This may be stated simply as being *"instantaneous, complete, and final"* (A. H. Strong). It must be *instantaneous*, for there can be no neutrality in our relationship with God; he either counts us his enemies or his friends (Mt 12:30). It must be *complete*, for, as Judge, God must pronounce us either guilty or not guilty (Ac 13:38-39). And it must be *final*, for there can be no true joy in a salvation that is here today but gone tomorrow (Jn 10:28; Ro 8:28-39).

But I do rejoice, because I know that justification is maintained in me, even if I should happen again to fall into sin. My assurance of this lies in the high priestly ministry of Christ. As far as mankind in general is concerned, the one death of Christ on the cross has made an all-sufficient atonement for all sin (He 9:26,28). But this sacrifice is made efficacious to me personally only when I actually show faith in Christ, and when he, as my great high priest, intercedes for me before the Father (see He 2:17; 4:14-16; 7:24-25).

Further, while justification must logically be antecedent to the life-giving work of regeneration and the moral work of sanctification, in actual fact justification and regeneration are concurrent. That is stated in numerous places where the legal declaration and the moral act are closely linked (see Ro 8:30; 1 Co 6:11; Ep 5:25-26; 1 Pe 1:2).

FULL ASSURANCE OF JUSTIFICATION

In two powerful sentences the scriptures urge upon you the benefit of letting your heart be fully assured of your position before God. In the first Paul speaks of the riches that will be yours if you permit your understanding of your position to lead to a deep inner assurance -

> *I am struggling on your behalf, so that you may be encouraged in spirit and united in love, and that you may possess all the riches of assured understanding. I want you to know the mystery of God, namely Christ, in whom are hidden all the treasures of wisdom and knowledge* (Cl 2:1-3).

In the second the apostle shows how this full assurance will lead to vigorous faith and a bold approach in prayer -

> *Therefore my friends, since we have confidence to enter the Most Holy Place by the blood of Jesus, let us approach God with a true heart in full assurance of faith, and let us hold with unswerving faith to the hope we profess, for the One who promised is faithful* (He 10:19-23).

So let this full assurance of faith grip you. Having believed, it is imperative that you should know yourself to be fully justified in Christ. Be perfectly persuaded that you are redeemed, that you have eternal life, that you will never perish, that God cannot fail to keep you and to complete his purpose in your life. Be settled in your mind, convinced in your heart, once and for all, that you are a child of God. Know that none can remove you from the Father's family: you are his by adoption, you are his by regeneration!

Nothing less than this full assurance of justification will enable you to experience full joy, full confidence before God, full victory over sin and Satan, and to press on into the full measure of the stature of Christ!

CONCLUSION

And now, having written all those words to explain the meaning of *"justification"*, I am bound to admit that Andrew Faussett managed to tell the whole story marvellously well in just one sentence -

> "We are justified judicially by God, meritoriously by Christ, instrumentally by faith, evidentially by works!"

CHAPTER THREE:
REDEMPTION

> *"We have redemption through his blood, the forgiveness of sins"* *(Ep 1:7).*

I once read a book on the power of the blood of Christ. It dealt particularly with a practice the author called *"pleading the blood"*, and it endeavoured to establish that those who *"pleaded the blood"* would find themselves invincible against Satan.

Many scriptures were quoted, and many fine thoughts were presented, especially when the author stressed the value the blood has in making atonement for our sins and in creating peace between man and God.

But he went beyond scripture when he tried to present the *actual* blood of Christ as a weapon we can personally use in our spiritual warfare. That part of his book reflected pagan superstition more than it did the gospel of Christ. It left an impression that the blood of Christ is a kind of lucky charm, able by itself to ward off evil; it tended to reduce the atonement to the level of superstition, rather than exalt it into the realm of faith; it claimed that we still had access to the physical blood that Jesus lost at Calvary.

The author showed a great fondness for expressions like

>plead the blood against the devil
>draw a blood line
>nothing can cross the blood line
>stretch out your hands and sprinkle the blood
>put your mind under the blood
>cover yourself with the blood
>- and so on.

On the face of it, those expressions might seem harmless enough - but that depends on how they are used.

If they are used figuratively to imply no more than an appropriation by faith of the benefits of the atonement, then they may well be helpful. But if they are used (as they were by the author of that book) to mean a literal and factual contact with the actual blood Christ spilled twenty centuries ago, then they are plainly misleading.

This practice of *"pleading the blood"* contains a grave danger: when people have drawn around themselves the so-called blood line (although how such an intangible, mystical feat can be actually performed is left unsaid) they tend to sit back and relax in false security, imagining within themselves, *"Nothing can get past the blood!"*

But such an attitude is hardly warranted by scripture, which gives a very different picture of the place the blood of Christ has in the program of salvation -

WHERE IS THE BLOOD OF CHRIST

It is clear that we cannot have any direct contact with the blood of Christ. It is not sprinkled on us, and we cannot sprinkle it anywhere ourselves.

Back in the days of ancient Israel there were two primary places where the blood was found:

> *on the altar of sacrifice (Le 17:11);*
>
> *on the mercy-seat in the* "holy of holies" *(Le 16:14).* [12]

Today we find our altar and our mercy-seat in the cross of Christ:

> *We have an <u>altar</u> . . . (where) Jesus suffered outside the gate so that he might make his people holy through his own blood* (He 13:10-13). And again: *(We) are justified*

---

[12] The altar and the mercy seat are described in Ex. 25:8-10, 17-21; 27:1-8; see also, 37:1-9; 38:1-7. Note also that there were some special occasions when a symbolic sprinkling of the blood upon the people did occur (eg. Ex 24:8; He 9:9,13), but it is improbable that every citizen was sprinkled. Presumably the sprinkling was restricted to a smaller group of representatives. In any case, for us the gamut of Mosaic sacrifices are brought together in Christ; and more particularly, in connection with the great Day of Atonement, there was no sprinkling of the people (see Le 16).

> *freely by his grace, through the redemption that is in Christ Jesus, whom God has presented as <u>an atoning sacrifice</u> by his blood, which we must receive by faith* (Ro 3:24-25).

In the latter reference, *"expiation"* is *"hilasterion"* in Greek, which is directly linked with the OT idea of *"the mercy seat"*, the place where the blood of atonement was sprinkled in the temple. The same Greek word is, in fact, translated *"mercy seat"* in *Hebrews 9:5*.

So our *altar* and our *mercy seat* are brought together at the one place: *Calvary*.

Furthermore, the apostle shows (in *Hebrews 9*) that *all* of the old sacrifices and blood-sprinklings specified by Moses are embraced in the Cross. For us, then, there is only *one* sprinkling of the blood, and only *one* place of sacrifice. We search no further than Calvary for full salvation.

Now the offering by Christ of his own life as an atonement for our sins has occurred *once only* in history, and will never occur again (He 9:25-28). Once, at the end of the old dispensation, Christ gave himself and surrendered his life as an expiation for human sin. We now look back in faith, we see the blood sprinkled on Calvary's altar, and we know that total atonement has been made.

However, from Gods' point of view, Jesus is *"the Lamb slain from the foundation of the world"* (1 Pe 1:19-20; Rev 13:8, AV). In the eyes of God the death of his Son is eternally present; for there is always an image in heaven,

> *in the very middle of the throne, of a Lamb still bearing the marks of slaughter upon him* (Re 5:6).

In that spiritual sense the blood maintains an eternal witness in heaven that atonement has been made, and Calvary is continually presented to the Father as our *"mercy seat"*.

So we have a double answer to the question, *"Where is the blood?"* First, the blood of Christ has once been shed on the cross, in an act that is historically past and completed. Second, because God dwells in eternity, not time, to him the sprinkling of the blood is an ever-present fact, and the cross is perpetually revealed as the altar to which we may come for pardon and mercy.

Nonetheless, from our human point of view, no actual contact with the blood of Christ is possible. Some of his blood perished in the dust of Golgotha, some of it stained the timbers of the whipping post and the cross, what remained was transformed in the resurrection. But his original blood in itself was no more eternal nor indestructible than his saliva or sweat (which were also torn out of him during his passion). The significance of the blood of Christ to us does not depend upon us being able in some kind of literal sense to *"sprinkle"* it upon ourselves - which in any case is manifestly impossible.

That leads us on then, to explore the real meaning of the blood.

THE VALUE OF THE BLOOD

What value does the blood of Christ hold for us?

That question may be answered by looking at several key passages -

THE LIFE IS IN THE BLOOD

> *The life of the flesh is in the blood; and I have given it to you so that you may put it on the altar to make atonement for your souls. Because of the life that is in it, the blood will make an atonement for you* (Le 17:11).

The blood is peculiarly appropriate as an agent of atonement, because in a vital sense the blood is the vehicle of life for the whole body - *"the life of the flesh is the blood."* To shed the blood, then, means to offer the *life* of the sacrificial victim; or perhaps better, to present the victim's *death* as proof that full expiation has been achieved.

From earliest times blood has been dignified as the embodiment of life. God said to Noah,

> *You must not eat flesh with its life, that is, its blood, still in it* (Ge 9:4). And again, *Be sure that you do not eat any blood; for blood is life, and you must not eat the life with the flesh. You shall not eat it. Instead, you will pour it out upon the earth like water* (De 12:23-24).

This use of *"shedding blood"* as a metonym for death is seen in many places in scripture. For example, Jeremiah castigates the wicked: *"On your skirts is found the blood of innocents"* (Je 2:34; 19:4). Innocent people had been murdered, their lives had been taken, and perhaps their blood shed. For the unjust death of those people the Lord exacted vengeance.

The same principle was taught to Noah:

> *For your lifeblood I will surely require a reckoning. From every one of you I will require the life of your neighbour. Whoever sheds the blood of someone, by someone else shall their blood be shed; for God made men and women in his own image* (Ge 9:5-6).

In that reference, the phrase *"whoever sheds the blood of someone"* is obviously synonymous with murder, or taking someone's life, whether or not that person's death actually involves loss of blood. In the law of Moses also, it is plain that *"shedding blood"* is synonymous with *"putting to death"*, and that actual loss of blood is not necessarily implied:

> *If anyone kills a person, as established by the evidence of reliable witnesses, then the murderer must be put to death. Moreover you must not accept any bribe for the life of a murderer. If he or she deserves the death penalty, then capital punishment must be imposed. Blood pollutes the land, and you cannot rid the land of the guilt it carries because of the blood that was shed on it, except by shedding the blood of the murderer (Nu 35:30-33).*

Thus atonement does not consist of the offering of some mystical life contained in the blood itself (as some have argued), but rather of the *presentation* of the blood as proof of the *death* of the sacrifice. The blood itself does not possess any kind of inherent or independent life; rather, it is an expression of *"the life of the flesh"*, and the outpouring of the blood means the outpouring of the life of the sacrifice. But because the blood is co-extensive with the whole body, carrying life to every cell of the body, it can properly be called *"the life of the flesh"*, and it is therefore especially suitable as a representation of the surrender of that life.

So, atonement for sin was gained, not just by sprinkling a little of the blood of a living sacrifice, trusting in some peculiar life-power in that blood to bring redemption, but rather by *killing the sacrifice* and by offering all of its blood as *evidence of its death.*

Thus atonement required more than just the *sprinkling* of the blood; it involved the *presentation* of a complete sacrifice to God (cp. Ex 29:31-33), and the basic purpose of the sacrifice was *substitution.* The blood, as the life of the flesh, showed that an innocent victim had suffered death in place of a condemned sinner.

The whole transaction stems from God's decree that blood poured upon his altar, as a witness of the sacrificial death of an appointed victim, will be accepted as a substitute for the death penalty that should rightly have fallen upon the sinner. The blood guarantees that adequate atonement has been made for our souls (Le 17:11).

THE BODY AND BLOOD OF JESUS

See John 6:51-56, 60-63.

At first hearing, those words of Jesus are hard to receive. It is not surprising to find that

> *the Jews then fell into furious debate with each other, arguing, "How can this man give us his flesh to eat?" Even his disciples when they heard it, said, "This is a hard saying; how can anyone receive it?"*

In fact, so outrageous was it to hear a man talking about others eating his flesh and drinking his blood, that *"many of his disciples turned away from him, and no longer went about with him"* (vs. 66).

The Lord knew that his disciples were murmuring about his saying. He said to them, *"Are you offended by what I said?"* (vs. 61). Then he explained to them how his words should be understood. He said,

> *It is the spirit that gives life, the flesh brings no profit at all; but the words I have spoken to you, they are spirit and they are life* (vs. 63).

That is, the saying about eating his flesh and drinking his blood, must be read figuratively, not with crude literalness. It must be read against the background of his true identity as the eternal Word of God (Jn 1:1-3). His true *"flesh"* and *"blood"*, or at least the real values of his human form, are conveyed to us by the word he has spoken - his *words* are the real source of spiritual life.

So the expressions *"eating his flesh"* and *"drinking his blood"* are simply a very graphic way of saying that we must enter by faith into the benefits of his death on the cross. But since we are completely dependent on his own witness that his death was not merely that of a martyr, but an eternal sacrifice in which he gave *his* life as a ransom for *ours* (Mt 20:28; Mk 10:45), to *"eat"* and *"drink"* Christ effectively means, *"believe the word he has spoken"*. His word alone exposes the real significance of his life, death, and resurrection.

So he said,

> *I am the living bread that came down from heaven; if any one eats of this bread, he will live forever; for indeed, the bread that I will give for the life of the world is my flesh* (vs. 51).

That is an obvious reference to his coming death at Calvary, and it explains the meaning of the *"bread"*: it is the benefit obtained for us by the Lord's death on the cross. And how do we gain access to that benefit? Just by faith in Jesus himself and in the word of life he has spoken: *"Very truly, I tell you, whoever believes in me has eternal life"* (vs. 47,63).

Once again you will see that eternal life does not lie in the power of the blood alone; rather, it springs from the fact that the blood represents the atoning death of Christ. His body was torn, his blood was shed, he gave his life for the world. The infinite value of that life provides an infinite redemption for mankind. But each one of us can participate in that redemption only when we each know and believe that Jesus died for us, and when, by faith, we each appropriate to ourselves the benefits of that death.

PROPITIATION BY THE BLOOD

See Romans 3:24-26.

The blood sprinkled at Calvary designates Jesus as the eternal *"mercy-seat"*, the heavenly equivalent of ancient Israel's place of propitiation (cp. Le 16:14).

The mercy-seat was the gold lid that covered the ark of the covenant. It was placed in the innermost part of the sanctuary (the holy of holies) where the high priest was permitted to enter only once a year. On that day, the great day of atonement, the high priest parted the veil and sprinkled the blood of the sacrifices on the mercy-seat. When this was done, the wrath of God was appeased and Israel was reckoned to be redeemed from all sin.

For us, the ancient type is fulfilled in our anti-type, Jesus. Through the cross, and by his resurrection and ascension, Jesus has become our sacrifice, our altar, our mercy-seat, and our high priest (see *Hebrews 9*).

Paul declares that God has put Jesus forward *"as an expiation by his blood"*. I have already mentioned that the word translated *"expiation"* is used as the Greek equivalent of the Hebrew word for *"mercy-seat"*, and it means *"the place of reconciliation"*, or *"the place of propitiation"*. It reveals the expiatory nature of the death of Christ: he died to pay the debt we owe God by our sin.

In particular, that propitiation was achieved by the shedding of the blood of Jesus, in fulfilment of the type, which designates the cross as our mercy-seat. The Amplified Bible reveals these things in its rendering of the passage:

> *All are justified and made upright and in right standing with God . . . through the redemption which is provided in Christ Jesus, whom God put forward before the eyes of all as a mercy-seat and propitiation by his blood - the cleansing and life-giving sacrifice of atonement and reconciliation - to be received through faith.*

Two things are made clear -

- ➤ *First*, there is an inseparable parallel between the death of Christ and the death of the sacrifices of old, so that we can speak of his blood as the source of our redemption - a redemption far beyond anything that could be offered by the blood of bulls and goats.

- ➤ *Second*, the benefits of the cross must be received by faith - not faith in the blood itself, but rather faith in the *complete redemptive act* that was wrought by the death, resurrection, and ascension of Christ.

Two specific benefits are gained by presenting Calvary as the place of propitiation -

> (1) It proves that God acted with *justice* when he showed *forbearance* toward sin during the centuries before Christ died (vs. 25).

That proof was necessary, because the Divine patience and tolerance during this period, right up to our own day, has laid God open to the charge of partiality and injustice. But now, says Paul, the shedding of the blood of Christ has revealed both God's fierce judgment against sin and the rightness of his actions. God did not after all tolerate wickedness. His longsuffering was not a sign of weak pity, nor of ineffectual judgment. The horror of the Cross is the measure of God's hatred of iniquity and of his resolve that no sin will be merely excused. Justice *has* been done. The violated law has been requited. Divine vengeance is satisfied. All in the person of the innocent Victim who willingly died in our place.

> (2) By his death on the cross Christ created a *redemption* that enables God freely and fairly to *justify* the believer.

"Redemption" means *"to release by payment of a ransom."* In our case, the death of Christ is the ransom that has purchased liberty for us who were slaves to the guilt and power of sin. That in itself would be a gift wonderful enough. But there is a further result of Calvary that goes far beyond the simple idea of *"ransom"*. Not only has the Cross brought us liberty, it has also enabled God justly to *"justify"* us - that is, to treat us as though we have *always* been innocent and fit to stand before him as righteous persons.

We who believe are therefore much more than just emancipated slaves, or pardoned criminals. We have been brought into the position of people who never were slaves, who have never been under any shadow of guilt, and who therefore enjoy the unsullied rights and privileges of free-born citizens.

These incredible gifts become ours the moment we believe in Christ. God asks nothing more, he will permit nothing more (nor anything less), than plain faith. We are required simply to trust in the full sufficiency of the ransom Christ has provided. Having done so much for us, the Saviour rightly demands contentment with his merits alone. So let us be done with any and all efforts to make our own atonement! The Cross is enough to satisfy the most rigorous demands of God's offended law.

RANSOM BY THE BLOOD

See Hebrews 9:12.

In almost every case in the NT the words *"ransom"*, *"redeem"*, and their derivatives, are based on the Greek word *"lutron"*, which means, *"the price of release (from debt, bondage, or punishment)."* As an extension of this, *"lutron"* sometimes means the deliverance itself, the idea of a ransom being actually ignored - see, for example, Lu 21:28; He 11:35. However, the normal meaning of *"lutron"* is simply that of paying a ransom.

In scripture, no mention is made of the recipient of the ransom price. The thought behind *"redeem"* is not so much a price paid to another, as it is the idea of a substitutionary death. The ransom price is specified - death. However, *"Christ gave himself,"* not *to* someone, but rather *for* us. Thus we read -

> *The Son of man came . . . to offer his life as a ransom for many* (Mt 20:28). *Jesus Christ . . . gave himself for us to ransom us from all iniquity* (Tit 2:14).

Because of these things, our text (He 9:12) declares that by his own blood Jesus has become our eternal high priest, and that having obtained full redemption for us, he has entered the holiest to *"appear in the presence of God on our behalf"* (vs. 24-26). His blood, sprinkled on the mercy seat before the Father in heaven, is now the *"lutron"* that has purchased release for us from the *debt* we owed God, from the *punishment* that was due to us, and from all spiritual *bondage*. Therefore our text continues -

> *The blood of Christ . . . (will) wash your conscience clean of dead works so that you may serve the living God (vs. 14).*

The ransom is paid to rid us of the penalty and guilt of our transgressions, which then releases us to live for God, to come boldly into his presence, and to receive the promise of everlasting life (vs. 15; see also Ep 1:7; Cl 2:14).

We read also that by the shedding of blood we receive *"forgiveness"* of sins (vs. 22). A different Greek word is used here, which like *"lutron"* means *"to set free from debt or punishment,"* but without any idea of a price being paid. The idea here is rather that of the very cause of the offence being removed, so that pardon is automatic. The same word is used in *Matthew 26:28,*

> *This is my blood of the new covenant, which is poured out for many to bring forgiveness of sin.*

So the first part of redemption is pardon - a pardon based upon both a removal of the source of our guilt, and a release from the penalty of it. But the second part, as we have seen, is victory - about which I will have more to say in a moment.

ACCESS BY THE BLOOD

> *See Colossians 1:20; Ephesians 2:13-16; Hebrews 10:19-22; 4:16.*

Those references all show the immense value of the blood: it provides for God the *legal basis* upon which he can justly pardon our sins, credit us with the righteousness of Christ, and then set us free to serve him in righteousness. That is the divine side. The human corollary is that the cross makes it possible for us to approach God boldly, without guilt or shame, trusting only in the merits of Christ, and so find grace and help in every time of need.

You will notice that *the scriptures do not speak of the blood itself as actually having power*. The power lies rather in the hand of God. The blood is powerful only in the sense that it provides a covering (*"atonement"*) for our sins, and thus gives God the legal right to act mightily on our behalf.

DELIVERANCE BY THE BLOOD

> *See 1 Peter 1:18-19; 1 John 1:7; Revelation 1:5; 7:14; 12:11.*

(1) Peter points to the likeness between the redemption given to us in Christ, and Israel's deliverance from Egypt. When God was about to judge Egypt and to deliver Israel from slavery, he commanded the Israelites to sprinkle the blood of a lamb over their doorways (Ex 12:7). Then the Lord told the people that the

angel of death, "the Destroyer" would go through the land of Egypt and kill the first-born of every household; but the Lord promised that he, too, would go through the land, and whenever he saw the blood he would "pass over" that house and protect it from the plague (Ex 12:12-13,23).

It is important to see that the blood, by itself, actually had no power against the Destroyer. The blood alone could not have saved any family. The angel of death would not have been hindered for a moment by a few splashes of blood. It was not the <u>angel</u> who "passed over" the houses where the blood was sprinkled, it was the <u>Lord</u>. When God saw the blood, <u>he</u> "passed over" that house, wrapped it around with his mighty power, and so prevented the Destroyer from entering.

That same principle applies to the blood of Christ.

We take our stand upon the fact that Jesus' precious blood was sprinkled on "the mercy-seat" before the Father at Calvary. We claim this sprinkled blood as our own; it is the blood of our sacrificial Lamb (Jn 1:29; Re 5:6-10). Seeing our faith in the blood, the Father is drawn to "pass over" us, to protect us from the enemy, and to make available all of his mighty resources.

> (2) You will see then that the blood does not challenge or oppose Satan (as some have supposed); rather, it speaks to God (He 12:24). We present the blood of Christ by faith, not to the devil, but to the Father.

By itself, the blood has no strength to drive off the devil. But it does provide the ground upon which we may stand in the righteousness of Christ, and by which God is then able to stretch out his own hand to bring us deliverance.

The blood of Christ is therefore not a weapon, neither of attack nor defence; it is simply the basis of your redemption, the ground upon which you stand when you approach God. The blood cannot protect you, but God can and will, because of the blood.

Likewise, the blood cannot give you victory, but it does enable God to impute to you the righteousness of Christ (Ro 4:22-25). That righteousness then becomes the basis upon which you gain free access to the invincible spiritual weapons that have been given to you.

What are those weapons?

They are three: the powerful name of Jesus (Mk 16:17-18); the mighty promises of God (2 Pe 1:4); and the supernatural gifts of the indwelling Spirit (Ac 1:8; 1 Co 14:7-10).

Those weapons are more than sufficient to meet every need you may have, and they are mighty to pull down every stronghold of Satan (2 Co 10:4). But they are available to, and can be used by, only those who have been reconciled to God and who have found peace through the blood of the cross (Cl 1:20).

(3) Now we can see the significance of the statement,

They overcame Satan by the blood of the Lamb, and by the word of their testimony *(Re 12:11).*

Taking their stand upon the blood of Christ, and the freedom his blood gave them from the fear of death (He 2:14-15), the saints were able to take up the word of God (which is the Sword of the Spirit, Ep 6:17) and to triumph over all the works of the devil. The *word* was their *weapon*; the *blood* was the *ground* upon which they stood. And after all, any weapon is only as good as the position from which it is used!

It may be noticed here that the preposition *"by"* does not mean *"by means of"*. In the Greek text *"by"* is *dia*, which can be used in two different ways. Depending on the grammatical structure of the sentence *dia* may mean either *"by means of"* or *"as a result of"*. Here is an example of each use: *"he spoke (by means of) a parable"* (Lu 8:4); and *"I have written to you (as a result of) the grace given to me by God."* (Ro 15:15).

The form of the Greek in *Revelation 12:11* requires the second reading, so that *"by the blood"* means *"as a result of the blood"*, or *"because of the blood"*. The whole passage then means, because of their testimony of faith in the blood of the Lamb, the saints received strength from God to resist and overcome Satan (cp. 1 Pe. 5:8-9). The blood itself is not the means by which we gain the victory, but because of the blood we can stand in Christ and draw on his strength to overcome the kingdom of darkness.

(4) Let me add a few more comments on the nature of the blood of Jesus. It seems to me that a chemical analysis of his blood (if it could have been made during his lifetime) would have shown it to be ordinary human blood - as indeed a chemical analysis of

his flesh (or of any part of his body) would have shown it to be ordinary human flesh. That is surely a necessary corollary of the doctrine of the incarnation. As Paul wrote:

> *(Jesus) was born in the likeness of a human being, and was fashioned as a man* (Ph 2:7-8).

In other words, he was not a pseudo-man; his manhood was not a pretense; his humanity was not some kind of camouflage thrown over his divinity. He was truly and genuinely human, except for two distinctions: he was without sin; and behind his human identity there remains his unchanging identity as the eternal Word. That has always been orthodox Christian doctrine.

Our very salvation depends upon the fact that Jesus was actually death has efficacy for me, another man; as *Son of God*, his death has efficacy for the whole race of man. If he were only divine, his sacrifice would have no relevance to humanity (cp. He 2:14-18). If he were only human, his sacrifice could do no more than save one other human. Humanity and divinity must both be in him fully if his death is to have power to save all who believe.

Nonetheless, during the years of his incarnation he did not walk among us in the garb of humanity, like a deity in disguise, with his seeming manhood nothing more than an illusion. He really was a man, in every sense of the word.

If that is so (and it has for centuries been the common belief of Christians), then it becomes clear that the blood of Jesus has no power in itself. Once again, the phrase *"the blood"* is shown to be simply a synonym for life or death. The value of Calvary lies not in the fact that Jesus lost some blood there (blood that presumably changed into the dust with which it mingled), but that *"he yielded his life as a ransom for us all."* It is the giving of his *life* that has created for us a sure hope of victory over death.

To *"plead the blood"*, then, is really only a particular way of affirming confidence that *"Jesus died for our sins and rose again for our justification."* In actual fact, our trust is not in *"the blood"* as such, but rather in Jesus' death and resurrection. So when the blood of Christ is mentioned in scripture, it should mostly be understood simply as a vivid metaphor for all that the cross and the empty tomb represent to the eye of faith.

It is sometimes claimed that *"the Holy Spirit contributed the blood of Jesus; therefore it is sinless blood, it is divine blood."*

If such statements are intended to be taken literally (rather than symbolically) then I must disagree with them. There is no way to prove that the Holy Spirit gave blood to Jesus in Mary's womb in a way peculiarly different from the giving of his flesh. That is a fanciful notion, with neither biblical nor biological support.

In any case, if Jesus' blood was sinless, so also was his flesh; if his blood was divine, so also was his flesh. But neither proposition is strictly true. It is *Jesus* who is sinless; it is *Jesus* who is divine. *Christ* is our redeemer. In *him* we place our trust. Such expressions as *"his blood"*, *"his cross"*, *"his flesh"*, and so on, are in the end just figures of himself.

So the real value of the blood lies in this: it is awful proof that an innocent Victim was brutally slain, and that a proper sacrifice for sin has been made. When that witness is presented to the Father by a contrite and believing heart, it provides a righteous basis upon which God can first pardon the believer, and then act in majestic strength to answer the believer's prayers, to bring marvellous deliverance, and to do all that an omnipotent God is free to do for his own dear child!

WASHED IN THE BLOOD

A question might now arise: what about the passage that says, *"they washed their robes and made them white in the blood of the Lamb"* (Re 7:14). Doesn't that show we *do* have direct contact with the blood?

> (1) The blood of Christ is not some vague, ethereal, mystical, limitless substance. It is not endless in supply or quantity. It was the actual, literal blood that flowed in the veins of Jesus of Nazareth. It is manifestly impossible for *one* person, let alone *millions*, literally *"to plunge beneath the crimson flood,"* or to *"wash his robes in the blood."* Those expressions, and others like them, must be taken as striking figures of speech; they are merely a graphic way of describing the cleansing God gives us because of the blood.

(2) Consider the Old Testament types. Nowhere in the rituals and sacrifices of Israel did anyone actually wash himself, or his garments, in the blood that was shed on the altars. But every godly Israelite knew well that when the blood was sprinkled on the altar, and on the mercy seat, God would see it, and the Lord himself would purge away their sins and make them clean. We may have the same confidence in God's response to the cross.

CONCLUSION

Knowing these things, let us have 'boldness to enter into the holiest by the blood of Jesus." His death and resurrection have created for us "a new and living way" into the presence of God. We can now approach the Father with "a true heart and with full assurance of faith," and we can grasp those spiritual weapons and divine resources that will meet our every need and make us more than conquerors in Christ! [13]

---

[13] You will find further comment on the main theories of the atonement in the Addendum, at the end of this series of lessons.

CHAPTER FOUR:

PREDESTINATION

"Are you an Arminian or a Calvinist?"

That is likely to be the first question some people will ask when you mention the word "predestination".

What would your answer be?

Or perhaps you would rather ask what my answer would be!

Actually, I am reluctant to be billeted in either of those camps; and I am fairly confident that the apostle Paul (if he were able to join in the debate) would also refuse to enlist on either side.

However, because of its importance in the history of Christian doctrine, the question really deserves a straighter answer than that. So let us see what better sense we can make of it.

Arminius and Calvin were two great scholars who chose two different ways to explain the method God uses to gather his church together. Both of them claimed to be Bible-based and to represent fairly the teaching of the NT. Both claimed Paul as an ally! Each insisted that in the end his view was the only true one. And across the centuries masses of Christians have been polarised around the one doctrine or the other.

John Calvin (1509-1564) was a French theologian who based his doctrines on two key ideas: the utter depravity of man; and the absolute sovereignty of God.

Jacob Arminius (1560-1609) was a Dutch theologian who emphasised human freedom of choice.

According to Calvin, we are saved by God's choice. According to Arminius we are saved by our own choice.

The issue is important, because it raises the questions: "Is salvation conditional, or unconditional? Once saved, is a person eternally saved? Or is it possible to fall away from Christ?"

Calvin would answer those four questions, "No, yes, yes, no!"

But Arminius would reply, "Yes, no, no, yes!"

The problem for us is, how would Paul answer them? That is what we will try to find out!

CALVIN? ARMINIUS? PAUL?

CALVINISM

Here is an outline of some of the chief tenets of Calvinism -

(1) The Lord God exercises an absolute and irresistible sovereignty over the entire universe and everything it contains, including man.

(2) That sovereignty is expressed in the decrees of God, by which he governs the universe and foreordains all things that come to pass. The divine decrees cover all of God's works, in creation and redemption, and they also embrace the actions of mankind, including human sin (although here the decree is reckoned to be permissive rather than causative).

(3) One group of decrees is related to predestination, which is defined as *"the plan of God respecting all of his moral creatures."* This plan is imposed on all men (good and evil alike), on the angels, on Satan, on the demons, and on Christ as Mediator.

(4) The presupposition that governs God's actions among men is the total depravity of the human race. Man is so incorrigibly corrupt that without God's direct help he cannot repent, believe, or make any choice toward God. The will of man is chained to evil, and only divine intervention can release men and women from the tyranny of sin.

(5) The first step in that intervention is the decree of *predestination*, which has two parts:

(a) ***Election***, which describes God's deliberate choice to save at least some of the human race in and by Christ; and

(b) ***Reprobation***, which describes God's fixed resolve to bypass the remainder of humanity and to refrain from granting them those special operations of his grace that bring the elect to repentance and faith.

(6) In so acting, God is not unjust, for he is under obligation to save no-one. All men have sinned by their own choice, and all deserve to perish forever. If God saves any, it is solely an expression of his grace and love.

(7) Since Christ has died only for the elect, and the purpose of the atonement would fail if any of them were to be lost, it follows that God must keep safe all those whom he has called to salvation. Hence arises the doctrine of *"the perseverance of the saints"* - that is, all of the elect will certainly be saved, being irresistibly drawn on to achieve their destiny in Christ.

(8) In summary, here is a passage from the writings of Calvin himself -

> . . . St Paul, to exclude all merit on man's part and to show that all comes from God's pure goodness and grace, says that he has blessed us according to his election of us beforehand . . . For the gospel is preached to some, while others do not know what it is but are utterly shut out from it, as if God should make it rain in one quarter but allow another quarter to remain very dry . . . Now if it is demanded why God pities the one part and forsakes and leaves and abandons the other, there is no other answer but that it so pleases him . . . What is the reason for this difference? Even this, that God directs the one sort by his Holy Spirit and leaves the other sort in their natural corruption . . . In short, we have to note here that we shall never know where our salvation comes from till we have lifted up our minds to God's eternal

counsel, by which he has chosen whom he pleased and left the remainder in their confusion and ruin. [14]

Each one of those eight points, of course, is bolstered by many scripture references; and it is generally admitted that in the Calvinist scheme there is an austere logic, a majesty, that is not matched by any other systematic theology. It therefore possesses a compelling appeal to many minds.

But does Calvinism truly reflect the message of the NT? Let us see what Arminius would say-

ARMINIANISM

(1) God is sovereign, in that he does all that he chooses to do, and none can withstand his will. But he himself has willed the freedom of man, thus man *is* able to act contrary to the divine purpose.

(2) The desire of God is that all men should be saved because Christ died for all (not just for the elect); but God cannot force salvation upon any person, for to do so would violate the freedom of choice he has given to mankind.

(3) Salvation is entirely a work of God, given freely, and with no dependence upon our good works or merits. Yet man has to fulfil certain conditions before he can gain this salvation. Some of those conditions are repentance, acceptance of God's grace, faith in Christ.

(4) Despite the strongest persuasion of heaven, each person remains absolutely free to reject the divine offer and to spurn the grace of God.

(5) The divine election is based on God's foreknowledge. In other words, God knows in advance who will not only embrace the gospel but continue to walk in faith, growing in grace and

---

[14] From a sermon by Calvin on Ephesians 1:3-4, partly reproduced in "The Christian Life," an anthology from Calvin, translated and edited by J. H. Leith; Harper and Row, San Francisco, 1984, pg. 84ff. See also pg. 94,95.

spiritual maturity, and *those* are the people he predestines to an everlasting inheritance. [15]

(6) No man is ever ordained to damnation, for the offer always remains open: *"Whoever wants to, may come!"*

(7) The saints can be sure of persevering only while they continue to use the means of grace God has provided, and thus maintain close fellowship with him.

Once again, many scripture references can be cited in favour of those Arminian doctrines. They undoubtedly reflect ideas that are taught in the Bible.

How then can they be reconciled with the equally scriptural ideas presented by Calvin?

It seems to me that Calvin's strong views on the sovereignty of God, and his interpretation of the meaning of predestination, are much nearer to scripture than the weaker views put forward by Arminius. But it is equally true that Calvin treats with disdain the substantial biblical evidence for human freedom of choice. In this, Arminius speaks more truly.

So we are faced with a problem that has perplexed many commentators. However, although it has gathered around the names of Calvin and Arminius, the problem did not begin with them. Indeed, the argument about predestination had raged for centuries before either of those theologians were born. Thus, that earliest and among the greatest of English poets, the whimsical Geoffrey Chaucer, published his *Canterbury Tales* around the year 1390 (about 150 years before Calvin

---

15 In the Arminian view, then, predestination does not precede the believer's confession of faith in Christ, rather, it results from that confession. Predestination is not a Divine initiative so much as it is a Divine response. Though it is wholly an act of Divine grace, not dependent on human merit, it nevertheless arises out of our salvation. We are not predestined to be born again; rather, because we have been born again we are predestined to inherit the kingdom of God. Predestination is a consequence of salvation, not the cause of it. By contrast, Calvin saw predestination as the effectual cause of salvation, and that without such Divine predestination no sinner would ever be saved.

wrote his *Institutes*). Included in the *Tales* is the story of a cock called Chanticleer, told by a priest, in which the priest makes this comment -

> But that which God's foreknowledge can foresee
> Must needs occur, as certain men of learning
> Have said. Ask any scholar of discerning;
> He'll say the Schools are filled with altercation
> On this vexed matter of predestination
> Long bandied by a hundred thousand men.
>
> How can I sift it to the bottom then?
> The Holy Doctor St Augustine shines
> In this, and there is Bishop Bradwardine's
> Authority, Boethius too, decreeing
> Whether the fact of God's divine foreseeing
> Constrains me to perform a certain act . . .
>
> Or whether a free choice is granted me
> To do a given act or not to do it
> Though, ere it was accomplished, God foreknew it,
> Or whether Providence is not so stringent
> And merely makes necessity contingent.
> But I decline discussion of the matter . . . [16]

It would be easy if we, like the nun's priest, could *"decline discussion of the matter."* But the problem will not so readily disappear; it is also too important to abandon so casually. So here is a more formal comment on the tension that does exist in scripture between these two: God's sovereign choice, and human free will -

---

16 The Canterbury Tales - translated into modern English, tr. by Nevill Coghill, Penguin Books, 1977, pg. 243,244. The selection comes from "The Nun's Priest's Tale." Augustine was bishop of Hippo in North Africa in the early 5th century, and one of the most renowned teachers of the Church. Bradwardine was archbishop of Canterbury in the early 14th century, and achieved great distinction in mathematics and divinity. Boethius flourished about 100 years after Augustine. He was a famous Athenian theologian and statesman. He wrote a treatise on philosophy, which included an extended section on predestination, which Chaucer himself had translated, and upon which he often pondered.

> That God's sovereignty in predestination is exercised consistently with man's perfect liberty to choose is an antinomy which it is impossible for us to reconcile, but which nevertheless, stands out clear in the teaching of (scripture). In Ro 9:20-21 St. Paul appeals to one side of the antinomy and affirms the Divine sovereignty by reference to the figure of the potter; and in Ro 10:11-15 he exhibits the other side when he affirms the universality and freeness of the gospel offer, saying, *"Whosoever shall call upon the name of the Lord shall be saved"* ... Whilst St. Paul ... affirms the doctrine of absolute predestination to life, he asserts no less clearly the truth of human responsibility. [17]

After reading such things, we are constrained to ask –

WHICH EMPHASIS IS MORE BIBLICAL?

Most commentators, as they endeavour to resolve this dilemma, tend to do so (as Calvin and Arminius did) by strengthening one side of the issue and weakening the other - so that divine sovereignty overwhelms human freedom, or vice versa. This is done even by writers who would refuse to wear either tag, Arminian or Calvinist.

Here are selections from two such commentators. You will have no difficulty determining which side they each favour, although each of them would probably deny adherence to a particular school of theology.

COMMENTATOR *"A"*

The scriptures do teach a predestination, but not that God predestines some to eternal life and others to eternal suffering. He predestines "whosoever will" to be saved - and that plan is wide enough to include everybody who really wants to be saved ... When the NT describes Christians as objects of God's foreknowledge, its purpose is to assure us of the fact that God has foreseen every difficulty that will confront us, and that he can and will keep us from falling ...

---

17 Hastings' Dictionary of the Apostolic Church, article, "Predestination." Baker Book House, Grand Rapids, 1973; reprint of 1918 edition.

Is salvation conditional or unconditional? Once saved, is a person eternally saved? The answer will depend on the way we can answer the following questions: On whom does salvation depend? Is grace irresistible?

> (a) On whom does salvation ultimately depend? On God or man? Certainly it must depend on God, for who could be saved if salvation depended on a person's own strength? . . . However, is there not a certain sense in which salvation does depend on man? The scriptures consistently teach that man has the power of freely choosing between life and death, and that power God will never violate.
>
> (b) *Can God's grace be resisted?* One of the fundamental principles of Calvinism is that God's grace is irresistible. When God decrees the salvation of a person, his Spirit draws, and that drawing cannot be resisted. Therefore a true child of God will certainly persevere to the end and be saved; even though he fall into sin, God will chastise him and strive with him. Speaking figuratively: the man may fall on the ship but he cannot fall overboard.

But the NT does teach that Divine grace may be resisted, and resisted to eternal loss . . . and that perseverance is conditional upon keeping in contact with God. [18]

COMMENTATOR *"B"*

The NT writers take for granted the OT faith that God is the sovereign Lord of events, and rules history for the fulfilling of his purposes. Their uniform insistence that Christ's ministry and the Christian dispensation represented the fulfilment of biblical prophecies given centuries before . . is proof enough of this. A new development, however, is that the idea of election (is) now applied, not to national Israel, but to Christian believers . . . The NT (represents) election as God's act of predestinating sinners to salvation in Christ "before the foundation of the world."

---

[18] Myer Pearlman, Knowing The Doctrines of the Bible, Gospel Publishing House, Springfield, USA. 1937. pg. 270, 271.

In John's gospel Christ says that he has been sent to save a number of particular individuals whom his Father has "given" him . . . These are his "sheep", his "own" . . . It was for them specifically that he prayed . . . He undertakes to "draw" them to himself by his Spirit . . . to give them eternal life . . . to keep them, losing none . . . to bring them to his glory . . . and to raise their bodies at the last day . . . The principle that those who enjoy salvation do so by reason of divine predestination is here made explicit.

. . . From all eternity, Paul declares, God has had a plan to save a Church, though in earlier times it was not fully made known . . . Believers may rejoice in the certainty that as part of his plan God predestined them personally to share in this destiny . . . The choice was wholly of grace . . . (and because) God is sovereign, his predestinating choice guarantees salvation . . .

It has been argued that God's foreknowledge is not foreordination, and that personal election in the NT is grounded upon God's fore sight that the persons chosen will respond to the gospel of themselves. The difficulties in this view seem to be: (a) this asserts in effect election according to works and desert, whereas scripture asserts election to be of grace . . . and grace excludes all regard to what a man does for himself . . (b) if election is unto faith (2 Th 2:13) and good works (Ep 2:10) it cannot rest upon foresight of these things; (c) on this view, Paul ought to be pointing, not to God's election, but to the Christian's own faith, as the ground of his assurance of final salvation . . . [19]

YOUR AUTHOR!

The impression left on me as I read these commentators, and others, is that they are moved to adopt either the Arminian or Calvinist system, not so much on the ground of scripture as on emotional or intellectual grounds.

Speaking personally, I find the Calvinist theology more compelling than the Arminian. To me, there is a consistency, a majesty, an awesome vision of God in Calvin's interpretation of scripture that is unmatched by

---

[19] From the article "Predestination", in The New Bible Dictionary; I.V.F., London, 1967; pg. 1025, 1026.

any other theology. Yet I know it is unsafe to adopt a doctrine just because it is emotionally satisfying, or intellectually acceptable.

The Lord himself warns:

> *For my thoughts are not your thoughts, and your ways are not my ways, says the Lord. For as the heavens are higher than the earth, so are my ways higher than your ways, and my thoughts than your thoughts* (Is 55:8-9).

So, although I lean toward Calvinism, I find the Bible keeps getting in the way!

Somehow the scriptures refuse to conform to our theories; they resist attempts to put everything into tidy compartments; they will not rest comfortably in the categories we create for them.

Hence I find myself obliged to accommodate - to retain as much of Calvin's view as I can; but also to allow the full force of many of the arguments used by Arminius.

Your inclination may of course be the reverse - to retain as much Arminianism as possible, but to yield often to Calvin's persuasion. Or perhaps you are able to live happily with both emphases, hopping from one to the other as the case requires!

That last position is more or less the one outlined in the following paragraphs.

A PRACTICAL SOLUTION

Myer Pearlman writes:

> The respective positions of both Calvinism and Arminianism are taught in the scriptures. Calvinism exalts the grace of God as the only source of salvation - and so does the Bible; Arminianism emphasises man's free will and responsibility - and so does the Bible. The practical solution consists in avoiding the unscriptural extremes of either view, and in refraining from setting one view in antagonism to the other. For when two scriptural doctrines are set squarely in opposition to each other the result is a reaction that leads to error. For example: over-emphasis of God's sovereignty and grace

> in salvation may lead to careless living, for if a person is led to believe that his conduct and attitude have nothing to do with his salvation, he may become negligent. On the other hand, over-emphasis of man's free will and responsibility, in reaction against Calvinism, may bring people under the bondage of legalism and rob them of all assurance. Lawlessness and legalism - these are the two extremes to be avoided. [20]

That statement is a fair one, although it is not altogether sound, for it fails to come to grips with several firm declarations of scripture. If Calvinists and Arminians are guilty of *over* emphasising *some* aspects of the argument, Myer Pearlman and others like him are perhaps guilty of *under* emphasising *every* aspect!

Pearlman speaks more truly when he writes,

> We are bound to be confronted with mystery as we set out to relate the mighty truths of God's foreknowledge and man's free-will. [21]

Surely that is the heart of the matter. We are dealing here with a subject where truly

> *our knowledge is fragmentary, for we are like people looking at a puzzle through cracked glass; at best our knowledge is only partial - but one day we shall see him face to face, and then we shall know fully even as we are fully known* (1 Co 13:9-12).

In the meantime, we must be content to hold onto all that scripture teaches, without compromising or weakening any revealed truth. If some of those truths do not seem to be logically compatible, then our sense of logic must yield, not the word of God.

Thus, if the Bible says that my salvation is dependent upon God's sovereign choice, and that he personally elected me in Christ before the

---

[20] Op. cit., pg. 273.
[21] Ibid.

foundation of the earth, then I am content to believe it and to rejoice in the eternal security conveyed to me by the Father's immeasurable mercy.

But if the Bible also says that salvation rests upon my own choice, upon a voluntary act of surrender to God, which I can choose to make or withhold, then I am content to believe that too, and to accept the solemn responsibility this places on me to hear and obey God's command.

The reconciliation of these apparently opposing ideas may be an intellectual problem, but it is no problem for faith!

POWERFULLY PREDESTINED

Here now are some of the basic and powerful ideas associated in scripture with predestination.

"PREDESTINATION" IS A SCRIPTURAL DOCTRINE

Some people talk as though *"predestination"* is a word invented by John Calvin, but absent from the Bible.

However, there are at least six different, frequently occurring words in the Greek NT that convey the idea of predestination. They are translated by such expressions as *ordained, chosen, elected, foreordained, called, predestined.* Those words are not fully synonymous, but they do all fit within the general framework of God's predetermined will concerning the salvation of his people.

A study of those words leads to certain conclusions that seem beyond dispute -

(1) Israel was a nation predestined to be the servant of God

> *What advantage then do the Jews have? . Much in every way! First indeed because they were entrusted with the oracles of God . . . To them belong an adoption as sons, along with the glory, the covenants, the giving of the law, the worship, and the promises . . . (They are) the people of God whom he foreknew . . . chosen by grace* (Ro 3:1-2; 9:4; 11:2,5. See also De 7:6; 14:2; 1 Sa 12:22; Ps 147:20; Am 3:2).

So it is apparent that God, as an act solely of his own will, by his own choice, apart from any human initiative, and in order to fulfil his own purpose, determined to raise up from among all the nations just *one* nation. That chosen nation happened to be Israel, but it could as well have been another. However, *which* nation was to be called was a matter for God alone to say.

An inevitable corollary of God's choice of Israel is that all other nations have had at least some limitations placed upon them -

> *When the Most High divided up the nations, when he scattered mankind over the earth, <u>he fixed the boundaries of each people</u> according to the number of the sons of God. For the Lord's share lies in his own people, Jacob is his chosen heritage* (De 32:8-9).

(2) If it is argued that it is unfair of God to choose one and not another, the scripture offers two replies -

    (a) God has an inalienable right to choose whom he will, without obligation to explain either his choice or the eternal purpose behind his choice.

God's right and God's purpose are declared in the following -

> *Whatever the Lord pleases he does, both in heaven and on earth* (Ps 135:6).

> *The Lord has made everything for its purpose, even the wicked for the day of disaster* (Pr 16:4).

> *Sovereign Lord, you are the Maker of heaven and earth, and the sea, and everything that exists . . and they must all do whatever your hand and your decree have predestined to take place* (Ac 4:24,28).

> *God shows mercy to whoever he pleases, and he hardens the heart of whoever he wills. You will say to me then, "How then can he blame anyone for what they do? For who can resist his will?" But who are you, a mortal, to answer God back?* (Ro 9:14-23).

    (b) Election by God brings commensurate responsibility, and threat of severe penalty for failure.

> *From everyone to whom much is given much will be required (Lu 12:47-48; 1 Co 9:16-18; Ja 3:1.)*

Nobody can bask in divine election, as though it is all privilege and no duty, for God makes high demands of righteousness and fruitfulness from those whom he calls to himself.

GOD CHOOSES HIS OWN SERVANTS

(1) Just as Israel was chosen from among the nations by an act of God's sovereign will, so some *individuals* have plainly been elected by God to receive his grace and to be enlisted in his service. For example: *Paul* (Ac 9:15); *Jeremiah* (1:4-5); *Cyrus* (Is 44:28; 45:1); the *twelve apostles* (Jn 15:16,19); and many others. That God chose those people, made his call irresistible, and caused them to persevere in his service, is indisputable.

This principle is demonstrated clearly in the life of Jeremiah -

> *Now the word of the Lord came to me: "Before I formed you in the womb I knew you, and before you were born I consecrated you and appointed you a prophet to the nations"* (1:4-5).

The prophet tried to evade that call and to withhold the word of God from the people; but the Spirit strove within him until he cried,

> *I am full of the (word) of the Lord; I can hold it in no more . . . Whenever I say, "I will never mention him again, nor will I ever speak again in his name," a fire starts to burn in my bones, his word boils in my veins until I can bear it no longer, and I must speak!* (6:11; 20:9).

Plainly, Jeremiah was singled out by God, and he was so powerfully prevailed upon by the Spirit that he virtually had no choice except to do what God commanded.

What is said of Jeremiah may be reasonably said of all who have been appointed by God to some special task - even those who, like Cyrus, were not conscious that they *were* doing heaven's bidding.

(2) <u>*Now this situation leads to certain conclusions*</u> -

    (a) It must be allowed that God is not only free to select and appoint his own servants, but that he *must* do so if there is to be any certainty of the fulfilment of his plan.

The mere existence of a divine plan requires God to choose beforehand the agents by which, or through whom, he intends to fulfil that plan, otherwise his purposes would constantly be at risk of being thwarted by human will.

So God declared he had known Jeremiah before the prophet was born, in fact, had personally fashioned him in his mother's womb.

Likewise, Paul recognised that God had *"set him apart before he was born, and had called him"* (Ga 1:15-16).

Without such a preselection of agents, and an effective calling, equipping, and keeping of them until their work is done, the success of God's plan would remain in constant uncertainty and jeopardy.

That no such threat to the plan of God exists, that there is no uncertainty about its success, is plain from scripture.

    (b) If it is fair for God to choose *one* person, to make that call irresistible, and to ensure that person's perseverance, then it is fair for God to choose *many*. But if it is unjust for God to elect *many*, then it is equally unjust for him to elect *any*.

But we have seen that it *must* be proper for God to predestine at least *some* per sons to do his will and to obtain eternal glory; therefore no limit can be placed on the exercise of his divine prerogative. He is free to elect all or none, few or many. He is Lord. He can do whatever he pleases, in heaven and on earth (Ps 115:3; 135:6; Is 46:10), subject to the rule of his own righteousness. But we have seen that it is not unrighteous of God to call irresistibly and solely by his own will at least *some* men and women to serve him. Furthermore, calling *some* (whether few or many) does not obligate him to call all.

THE CHURCH IS AN ELECT BODY

What is true of certain prophets, apostles, and other servants of God, as shown above, is stated in scripture as being true of the entire company of

God's people. Every believer is spoken of as being foreordained to obtain eternal life (see Jn 15:16; 6:37,44-45; Ac 13:48; Ep 1:4-5,11-12).

Just as it seems imperative for God to choose some people to *serve* him, it also seems imperative for God to choose some to be *saved*, otherwise Christ might have died in vain. (Not all who are obliged to serve God are recipients of his grace - remember Pharaoh, Caiaphas, and others.)

So Peter says: "You are a chosen race, a royal priesthood, a holy nation, God's own people" (1 Pe 2:9). And Paul establishes a very clear order in the way God deals with us when he writes: "Those whom God (1) predestined, (2) he also called; and (3) those whom he called he also justified; and (4) those whom he justified he also glorified" (Ro 8:30).

It does not say that God predestined those who are first justified. On the contrary, Paul is explicit that the reverse is true: *God justifies those whom he first predestined.* If justification preceded predestination, then we would have to say that the initiative for salvation comes from man. But if predestination precedes justification (as Paul claims) then the initiative is God's.

There seems then to be little doubt that *"predestination"* is predicated on God's actions, not ours. We are predestined, not because we chose Christ, but because God chose us. Predestination is not God's *response* to something we have done; rather, it is God's *routine* by which we are brought to repentance and faith.

THE GOSPEL INVITATION IS SINCERE

But having stressed the *divine* side of predestination (which has made me sound like a Calvinist), I must now stress another group of scriptures (which will make me sound like an Arminian!) But this next emphasis is just as much a part of the gospel as the first. And I believe it just as strongly.

> (1) **The Bible means what it says**: *"Whoever wants to, may come!"* (Re 22:17)

The call of the gospel to all men to repent, believe, and be saved, is *sincere* - anyone who chooses to respond to it may do so. It is always true that

> the Lord is not slack in fulfilling his promise, as some people might think, but is patient with us, not wanting

anyone to be lost, but giving time for all to come to repentance (2 Pe. 3:9).

The gospel is a genuine offer of salvation to any human being anywhere in the world who is willing to respond to God's love in Christ - *"whoever believes in him will not perish, but have everlasting life."* God loved the *world*, not just the *elect* (Jn. 3:16).

(a) Some commentators seek to lessen the difficulty by arguing that there is a basic core of elect people who comprise the foreordained foundation of the church, but that many others who choose to do so may also come and be joined with this group. They cite as examples

- the crowd of Egyptians and other foreigners who linked themselves with the elect nation of Israel at the time of the exodus (Ex 12:38). Zechariah appears to predict a larger re-enactment of that scene in the latter days, one that is already being at least partly fulfilled by the gentiles joining the church (8:23; and cp. Ro 11:1-2, 13-24).
- the young men who seized by faith the function of prophets in Israel (Nu 11:27-29).
- the unknown man who grasped a ministry of healing in the name of Jesus (Lu 9:49-50).
- the disciples who were not among *"the twelve"* whom Jesus had especially chosen, yet who were with him constantly from the beginning of his ministry (Ac 1:21-22).
- the words of Peter: *"I realise now that God has no favourites, but in every nation anyone who fears him and does what is right will be accepted by him"* (Ac 10:34-35).

(b) The problem is, this divides the church into two groups: the elect who are there because God chose them; and the remainder who are there by their own choice. This is hardly a satisfactory concept, because the scriptures include *all* the people of God when they speak of those who have been predestined, elected, called, and justified in Christ.

Probably any attempt to resolve the conflict will end in dilemma. It is best simply to accept that divine initiative and human responsibility are equal factors in our salvation - but where those two factors converge, how they can be harmonised, God has not yet revealed to us.

(2) *God and Man Act Together*

In the end I am content to avow that I would not be saved if the Father had not forcefully pressed me to repentance; yet I know equally well that the means of salvation was my personal confession of faith in Christ.

Human and divine action both played their part. God chose me. I chose Christ. Which choice was the more powerful I know not. I am content to let their meeting point remain like the cloud-topped peak of a high mountain, lost in the dizzying altitudes of God's inscrutable providence.

GOD USES MEANS

Divine election does not take place in a vacuum; it is not an abstract thing, removed from any tangible expression. God makes use of certain means to achieve his purpose, and our responses to those means, and our use of them, determine whether or not his election will become effective.

Paul wrote:

> *Before time began God chose you to be saved through the sanctifying work of the Spirit and through belief in the truth. That is why he called you through the gospel we preached, so that you might gain the glory of our Lord Jesus Christ* (2 Th 2:13-14).

Peter endorsed the same idea:

> *(You are) chosen in the purpose of God the Father, sanctified by the Spirit, and consecrated to Jesus Christ by the sprinkling of his blood* (1 Pe 1:2).

The task of *"sanctifying us by the Spirit"* may be God's, but the responsibility of *"believing the truth"* is ours! If he has *"called"* us, then it is *"through the gospel"*, and the call is made effective only by our *faith-response* to the gospel. We may indeed be *"chosen and destined"*, but we *enter into* the joy of that election by yielding to the Spirit's influence, by obedience to Christ, and by applying to ourselves the blood of redemption.

Further, the gospel, the blood, the Spirit, are freely available to *all* who seek the life of God in Christ. As we have seen, the gospel invitation is not a sham.

It is also plain that any who disobey the gospel, who despise the blood, who grieve the Spirit will be cast aside from God's grace. This is the next point -

IT IS POSSIBLE TO FALL AWAY

One of the main tenets of Calvinism is *"the perseverance of saints"*. That is, *"once saved always saved"*. It is impossible for an elect person to fall away from the grace of God. Yet that idea seems to be untenable in the light of many passages that warn against the perils of backsliding (see, for example, 1 Ti 1:19-20; He 3:12; 6:4-8; 10:26-31; 2 Pe 1:10-11; 2:20-22).

The usual Calvinist answer is this: none of the warning passages are addressed to truly regenerate persons, but in every case it must be assumed the persons concerned were not actually saved.

But that seems to be an evasion rather than an explanation. In fact, it tends to concede the point, that the warning passages unequivocally describe persons who have fallen away to perdition.

A plain reading of the warning passages satisfies most people they are addressed to Christians. To make those warnings applicable only to unbelievers empties them of any real meaning. Their sting is removed, their force is blunted. Worse, they become irrelevant, for unbelievers are already deeply condemned. Since they have never known Christ they can hardly fall away from him.

It seems awkward to accuse the apostles of such vacuity.

We are left with little choice except to agree (Calvin notwithstanding) that genuine Christians can, if they backslide seriously enough, find themselves cut off from salvation and condemned to an awful doom. The reason for that is because

LIFE IS IN THE SON

The most important statement in the NT is probably this one:

> *This is God's own witness: he has given us eternal life, and this life is in his Son. Anyone who has the Son has*

> *life; anyone who does not have the Son of God does not have life* (1 Jn 5:11-12).

"This life is in his Son!"

Your security is in Christ himself. If you cling to Christ you have life. If you cast him aside you lose life.

You may fail and fall often (as we all do), but so long as you maintain your trust in Christ, his life will prevail, sin will not have dominion over you, death will not seize you, and you will stand again to walk on with him.

Therefore, refuse to let go of Jesus, and you will always be able to say:

> *Do not rejoice over me, O my enemy; if I fall, for I will rise again. When I slip into darkness, the Lord will be my light. I may have to bear the anger of the Lord for a time, because I have sinned against him. But when he pleads my cause and enters into judgment for me, then he will bring me out into the light again; and I will experience his deliverance!* (Mi 7:8-9).

But if you give yourself to sin so carelessly that you lose all capacity for repentance and faith, if you grieve the Holy Spirit so deeply that he eventually flees from you, if you reach a state where there is nothing left in you that can keep a grip on Christ, then you will lose all remedy for sin. Nothing will remain but a terrible fear of the wrath of God.

But no one who has ever truly believed in Jesus can come to that dreadful condition easily or quickly. It is the result of a long process of constantly resisting the Holy Spirit and of constant rebellion against the will of God.

CONCLUSION

I have not shown you whether you should be an Arminian or a Calvinist. I do not even know which one I am myself! But I know this: *life is in the Son*!

I am his. He is mine. I don't intend to change my mind about him. I am sure he doesn't intend to change his mind about me!

There is no doubt about it: I have his life. Because of that life there is only one thing I can do: persevere until I have obtained the prize he has set before me (Ph 3:12-16).

He has predestined you to do the same.

CHAPTER FIVE:

SANCTIFICATION

Barry Chant writes:

> There is much confusion about sanctification. Most people misunderstand the basis of it - and missing this, they miss its whole purpose and blessing. [22]

He then goes on to define sanctification as:

> the act by which God separates believers from sin unto himself.

The NT writers employed several Greek words to convey the idea of sanctification. These words are usually variations of the root word *"hagios"*, and they are commonly translated either as *"sanctify," "holy,"* or their cognates.

Barry Chant gives the following list - [23]

hagios: holy - 161 (93 with *pneuma* = *"Holy Spirit"*)

                    holiest - 2

                    holiest of all - 1

                    holy one - 4

                    holy place - 3

                    holy thing - 1

                    sanctuary - 3

                    saint - 62 (61 in plural)

---

[22] From a set of unpublished lecture notes.
[23] Ibid.

hagiosmos:	holiness - 5
	sanctification - 5
hagiozo:	hallow - 2
	sanctify - 26
	be holy - 1
hagiosune:	holiness - 3
hagiotes:	holiness - 1

It will be readily seen that holiness and sanctification are identical in meaning.

The basic idea of both is separation. "Hagios" expresses separation from common condition and use. In Classical Greek, it had the idea of dedication to the gods, although it was rarely used outside of the New Testament. It was used to translate the Hebrew word "qadosh" which described things and people set aside for use in the tabernacle or temple. See Ex 29:44; etc. Christians are therefore set apart (from sin), for the service of God.

FURTHER DEFINITIONS

It could be said that the basic theme of the Bible is not salvation, but sanctification - that is, bringing men and women to holiness so that they may have fellowship with God (Is 33:13-17; He 12:14). Salvation is simply the first step toward that pursuit of holiness.

This is well-expressed in Paul's letter to the *Corinthians:*

> *"Therefore come out from among them and be separate from them, says the Lord, and touch nothing unclean; then I will welcome you, and I will be a father to you, and you shall be my sons and daughters, says the Lord Almighty." Since we have these promises, beloved, let us cleanse ourselves from every defilement of body and spirit, <u>and make holiness perfect in the fear of God</u>* (2 Co 6:17-7, RSV).

If we wish to be welcomed by God, to receive all the largesse he longs to pour out upon his own dear children, to have him *"live in us and move among us"* (6:16), then we must be (a) separate; (b) clean. Putting those two things together creates *"perfect holiness."*

Here then is the basic two-fold meaning of *"sanctification"*: *a holy object is either one that has been set apart for divine service, or one that is sacred in itself, or both.*

We lack a useful modern word to express that double meaning, but it was embraced well by the old English word *"hallowed"*, which is found in The Lord's Prayer: *"Hallowed be thy name . . . "* That is, *"Let thy name be set apart for sacred use alone;"* and, *"Let thy name be recognised as infinitely holy."*

To hallow, or sanctify, the Lord's name, means never to profane it, because it is *God's*, and always to reverence it, because it is *holy*. Here the outward state of separation, and the inward state of purity, are both clearly seen.

Sanctification, or holiness, therefore, may express an *outward condition*, or an *inward quality*, or *both*. Hence, a sanctified object may simply be one that is separated from one service and put to work in another. On the other hand, it may also be one that is purged of all profanity, and is made pure, becoming holy in itself.

Note also that an object (or a person) may be set apart for sacred use, and yet not be in itself sacred; or again, that an object may carry the quality of sanctity without being set apart for sacred purposes.

For a sanctified object that was not holy in itself see *Numbers 29:21*. For a holy object that was also sanctified (that is, set apart for divine service), see *John 10:36*. And for an expression of sheer holiness, without any commitment to service being involved, see *Exodus 15:11*.

So an object that is not inherently holy, but is separated for the service of God, and an object that is holy in itself, may both be spoken of as *"sanctified"*. But obviously, the full meaning of the word is not exhausted in such cases. *Total* sanctification appears only when those two elements are combined: namely, *when a separated object is made inherently holy; or when a holy object is used for sacred purposes.*

CHRISTIAN SANCTIFICATION

The full sanctification of a Christian involves each of the aspects outlined above. In effect, this means there are three steps in our sanctification:

- ➢ we are set apart for a holy purpose.
- ➢ we are made holy.
- ➢ we express this holiness in life.

It is important to understand those three steps, and especially to realise that the first two are wrought for us by God alone, while the third we must outwork ourselves. In brief, the Bible pattern of sanctification is this

- ➢ by the Holy Spirit we are separated from the world and brought to God.
- ➢ by Christ we are given a holy character.
- ➢ we must then set ourselves to practice holiness daily.

Here is an outline of those three steps -

SANCTIFICATION BY THE HOLY SPIRIT

Here we find the first, and basic meaning of *"sanctification"*: *something set apart for God.*

By God's own choice and command, the Holy Spirit separates the believer from the rest of humanity so that he might be saved. Two great passages of scripture declare this, and establish that the Holy Spirit has *already sanctified us* by setting us apart to be God's people -

(1) *We cannot stop thanking God for you, dear friends, beloved by the Lord, because before time began God chose you to be saved through the sanctifying work of the Spirit, and through your belief in the truth* (2 Th 2:13).

Here is sanctification wrought in us solely by the grace of God, who in his mercy caused the Holy Spirit to draw us to the place where we heard the gospel, believed the truth, and were saved. The result of this is that we have now been separated to serve God, and his goal is that we should *"obtain the glory of our Lord Jesus Christ"* (vs. 14).

> (2) *We have been chosen according to the foreknowledge of God the Father, by the sanctifying work of the Spirit, for obedience to Jesus Christ and sprinkling by his blood* (1 Pe 1:1, NIV).

The same pattern is found here as in the previous reference. Being elected to salvation by the mercy of God, that election was made effective when we were sanctified by the Holy Spirit. That is, the Spirit of God brought such influence to bear on our lives that we were separated from our fellows, brought to believe the gospel, and to trust in the sprinkled blood of Christ. This initial sanctification by the Spirit should naturally lead on to obedience to the truth; but if our obedience falls short because of human infirmity, there is provision for cleansing and restoration in the blood of Christ.

So here is an aspect of sanctification that is eternally complete. So far as heaven is concerned I bear a mark upon my life which testifies that the Holy Spirit has designated me for divine service. This mark may be defaced; the heavenly purpose may not be realised; but the essential fact can never be altered: *I am sanctified by the Spirit, set apart to serve God, ordained for sacred work.* Nothing can be added to that decree, nothing can be taken from it, it is complete, entire, finished forever (cp. Ro 11:29).

If you are a believer, then the same is obviously true of you.

You and I are *holy* because God has commanded us to be set apart for his service.

SANCTIFICATION BY THE LORD JESUS CHRIST

Here we have the second aspect of sanctification; not just being set apart from the world, but now *being made inwardly holy*. We move from a state of mere separation to the actual *quality* of sanctity or holiness. But this is still a sanctification that is given solely by grace, and, once given, is complete in itself. No work of ours can change this sanctification - no work, that is, except such as would root Christ out of our lives; for this impartation of holiness comes with Christ and cannot be separated from him.

> **(1)** *By the will of God we have been sanctified through the offering of the body of Jesus Christ once for all* (He 10:10).

It was the determined purpose of God to provide a means by which we could be sanctified; it was the willing choice of Christ to make himself that means.

> *Accordingly, we who now believe in Christ are truly sanctified; that is, we are given the righteousness of God, and are made a holy people, fit to serve the living God (1 Pe 2:9).*

See the finality of it: *"once and for all!"* It is done! The work is complete! We *are* sanctified! Holiness is freely given to us in Christ. The will of God is accomplished. Because we believe in the broken body of Jesus we are forgiven all our sin, and we are *made inwardly holy*.

> **(2)** *You are in Christ Jesus, who has become for us wisdom from God. He is now our righteousness, sanctification, and redemption* (1 Co 1:30).

Just as Christ is totally and freely made our redemption and righteousness, so he is also made our *holiness*. In him we are redeemed; in him we are also made holy. As certainly as salvation becomes our full and free possession immediately upon confession of our faith in Christ, so just as certainly, and at exactly the same moment, sanctification also becomes wholly ours.

If then you are saved, you are also sanctified; the one is equally complete as the other. They cannot be separated.

So, in connection with the work of the Holy Spirit, who separates you to believe and to serve the gospel, and in connection with the holiness of Christ, which is freely given to you through the cross, it may be truly said that you are *"entirely sanctified"*.

Nothing you can do can improve those perfect works of grace. By God's own decree all who believe in Christ become his separated servants and are sanctified in Christ. If you have believed, then you are holy.

So long as Christ is your Saviour, the fact of your full sanctification will remain firmly established.

However, the matter cannot be left there.

I have already mentioned that there is yet a third part of sanctification that we must work out ourselves. And this work a lifetime will not exhaust; neither will eternity be sufficient to complete it - for across the everlasting ages we shall always be rising higher and higher into the glory of God, being changed from glory to glory as we look on his face.

Toward this work let us bend our earnest attention -

APPLYING YOURSELF TO SANCTIFICATION
FOLLOW AFTER HOLINESS

If holiness has been accredited to you through Christ, it is for one reason only, that you might go on to live a holy life.

Two classic and deeply moving passages outline this advance into holiness:

> *Pursue that sanctification without which no one will see the Lord. Take care that you do not fail to obtain the grace of God . . . Do not be like Esau, who sold his birthright for a bowl of stew. For you know that afterward, when he wanted to inherit the blessing, he was rejected. He lost his opportunity to repent, though he sought for it with tears (He 12:14-17).*

We are commanded to "pursue that sanctification without which no one will see the Lord." The Greek word translated "pursue" has the sense "seek after (something) eagerly", or "earnestly follow (something)." The word means literally "to pursue without hostility." The idea is, that holiness is an eminently desirable goal, and one that we should press toward with all zeal. But it is also one that is unlikely to be fully attained in this life.

That is demonstrated by the associated noun, "peace." Says Paul, "Strive to be at peace with everyone, and for holiness." To live at peace with everyone is a godly ambition, and with proper effort one that may be nearly achieved. But is it possible to be utterly free of offence to any? Has anyone ever managed to have not so much as one enemy? Even the friendliest hearts anger some. Thus our quest for perfect peace is ultimately foiled.

The same may be said of the pursuit of holiness. This side of the resurrection, perfection of achievement is unattainable.

> *So Jesus suffered outside the gate, so that he might sanctify his people through his own blood . . . Therefore let us go out to him, outside the camp . . . For we cannot find here any lasting city, but we look instead for the city that is to come* (He 13:12-14).

Sanctification is given to us through the cleansing blood of Jesus. He suffered, we are sanctified. *"Therefore let us go to him outside the camp."* In that sentence the apostle gives a graphic picture of our position in relation to the cross. He paints a vivid scene of all the sanctified people of God dwelling within the city, surrounded by its walls, while outside, alone on the hill, is Christ on the cross.

As we watch this scene, a powerful plea comes that we, who have been sanctified by the crucified One, should leave the city, go forth to him, identify ourselves with Calvary, and share his reproach.

By the shedding of Christ's blood God has sanctified us; let us respond to this love by *sanctifying ourselves*. This we do by separating ourselves from the crowd in the camp, by taking up our cross to follow him, and by sharing in his shame. Thus we become citizens in his city.

We may exchange the casual camp for God's continuing city - but only by the way of the cross.

In brief: if God has sanctified you, you should sanctify yourself. If you have been set apart by the Spirit, then through the Spirit you should set yourself apart. If you have been called out by Christ, then go forth to Christ. If you have been made holy, then enter into holiness.

The message is clear. No Christian is exempted from it. God, having elected us by his grace, and having set his mark upon us to show that we are chosen to serve sacred things, now presses us to cooperate in this election, and to consecrate ourselves to live in the shadow of the cross. Having laid within us a sure foundation of holiness God now challenges us to erect on that foundation an edifice of holy living (1 Co 3:11-15).

Sanctification thus has a divine side and a human side. The divine work is complete. It is now our responsibility to bend our lives into conformity to the pattern established by God. Yet even here the success of our efforts depends on heaven's grace, for we go forth *"unto him"*, and only as we maintain our faith in Christ, and trust in the means he has provided, will our strivings be fruitful.

I want to guide you now in a more detailed study of this work of ...

CONTINUOUS SANCTIFICATION

A ship at sea with its engine out of order is in a desperate plight. If that ship is towed into port and fastened to the wharf it may be *safe*, but it is still not *sound*. Repairs may take many months. But when the repairs are completed the ship must venture again into the open sea. The object of bringing her into the harbour was not to keep her in useless idleness, but to make her sea-worthy, and to put her into service again.

Our case is similar. We are saved to serve. And we are fitted to serve by the process of sanctification.

Through *conversion* we receive God's pardon and are reconciled to him; we come into a relationship of grace. Then, through *sanctification*, we are linked with the vital life of God, so that intrinsic *holiness* may become extrinsic *righteousness*.

So people who have been truly saved should have within them a desire to be made spiritually whole, to be sanctified. The new birth should create a hunger for evil to be replaced by righteousness as the governing principle of life.

But though the inward corruption of the heart receives a severe blow at regeneration, pressures to do evil still remain, and at times they exert vigorous opposition to the work of the Holy Spirit. Before we were converted, sin reigned supreme; but now, though sin may no longer *reign* within us, it still *dwells* within us. Hence the possibility exists that it may once again exert control over us unless we co-operate with the sanctifying work of the Holy Spirit.

These three things, the continuity of the work of sanctification, the obligation we have to sanctify ourselves, and the ministry of the Spirit in sanctification, are taught in many places -

    (a) A continuous work: Ep 4:12-15; Ph 1:6; Cl 3:10; 1 Th 3:12; 1 Pe 2:2; 2 Pe 3:18.

    (b) Sanctify yourselves: Ro 6:12,19,22; Ph 3:12-16; 1 Th 4:3,4,7; 2 Ti 2:21; Tit 2:11-14; He 12:14.

This work requires us to bring ourselves diligently and willingly, body, soul, and spirit, into conformity to the pattern set by Christ (Ro 12:1-2; 13:14; 2 Co 10:5; Ep 5:1; Ph 2:12-13).

(c) <u>The ministry of the Spirit</u>: Ro 8:13-14; Ga 5:16; Ja 4:4-6.

This latter aspect of sanctification is discussed in greater detail below, section (III).

HOW CAN SIN REMAIN?

Many people find it difficult to understand how *"the lust of the flesh"* can remain in them after conversion. If Christ dwells in us, how can there be room for sin?

Yet the fact remains that all of us, despite the new birth, will fall again into sin. The apostle John included himself when he wrote:

> *If we say that we are without sin, we deceive ourselves, and there is no truth . . . If we say we have not sinned, then we make him a liar, and his word is not in us. My little children, I am telling you these things so that you may not sin; but, if any one does sin, then we have an advocate with the Father, Jesus Christ the righteous* (1 Jn 1:8-2:2).

Plainly, John is hoping that we won't sin, yet recognises that we will!

The solution to this problem lies in keeping a clear distinction between our *legal standing* and our *actual state*.

That idea is important enough to warrant a separate study, which you will find in your next chapter, *"Position."* In the meantime, let us explore the relationship between

HOLINESS AND LIFE

DEFINITION OF A HOLY LIFE

What does it mean to live a holy life? How can you determine whether or not you are living up to the biblical standards? What are those standards?

HOLINESS IS NOT

A STATE OF SINLESS PERFECTION IN THIS LIFE

Some Christians hold to the idea that it is possible to have a personal experience of sanctification that results in a state of *"sinless perfection."* This experience is sometimes called the *"second blessing,"* and after it has happened the Christian is reckoned to be *"entirely sanctified"*, and to be living without sin.

I do not enjoy denigrating a view sincerely held by some fine people of God, but in my opinion the idea of any person reaching in this life a state of complete freedom from sin is not supported by scripture. *"Sinless perfection"* is contradicted by the practical exhortations to holy living found in every NT letter. [24]

Many such references could be quoted, but two will suffice: *Galatians 5:16-17; 1 John 1:7-2:1*. Both of those passages take it for granted that the struggle against sin is an ongoing factor in the life of every Christian. Not that they deny the possibility of victory over sin - on the contrary, they assert that victory is possible - but they imply that sin will not be *completely* eradicated, it will remain present with the believer, and the believer is not removed from the possibility of yielding to it.

John Wesley (a great preacher of holiness) put it rather neatly: *"It is not impossible for a Christian to sin, but it is possible for him not to sin."* That seems to be the truth of the matter. We cannot expect to reach a place where every kind of sin, without exception, will become impossible for us; yet at the same time, in the face of temptation, there are more than enough resources available to us in Christ to resist and to overcome any particular sin. There is no necessity laid upon us to sin. Yet we do sin. Yet victory over sin is always available!

You will find a further explanation of the doctrine of *"entire sanctification"* just below (section IV); but for now, let us notice that holiness is not

LIVING BY A SET OF RULES

Many people think they are holy because they shun the picture theatre and dance hall, or because they do not smoke, or drink, or wear jewellery or cosmetics, or because they dress in a certain style, or avoid coarse forms of speech, and so on.

What a pitiful delusion! As Paul said, such rules and regulations, such *"laws"* of holiness, which say, *"Do not handle, Do not taste, Do not*

---

[24] See section (IV) for further discussion of this doctrine.

touch," are in the end self-defeating. They have an appearance of wisdom. They may seem to promote devotional rigour and humility. But it is a delusion.

A man-made *"holiness"* based on any kind of outward behaviour, or built out of negative prohibitions, has absolutely *"no value in checking the indulgence of the flesh"* (Cl 2:20-23). Quite the contrary, it *becomes* an indulgence of the flesh as it panders to the hunger of our fallen nature to establish a works-based claim upon God.

Furthermore, any *"holiness"* wrought by a set of human prescriptions will have a stifling effect upon the dynamic interaction the Holy Spirit desires to have with each believer.

Why?

Because from every person the Lord demands a different response.

For you the expression of his personal holiness may point in one direction, but for me it will point in another. From you the Lord may require a certain life-style, from me another. He moulds each of us in different ways; he designs each of us to show different facets of his own infinite beauty and glory.

The glory of the Pentecostal blessing is that it creates a holiness based on the inner working and leading of the Holy Spirit (which is unique for each person), and not upon a set of man-made instructions.

That is probably one of the basic meanings of *1 John 2:27* -

> *The anointing which you received from him remains in you, so that you have no need that any one should teach you; for just as his anointing teaches you about everything, and is true, and is not a lie, just as it has taught you, abide in Christ.*

We should respect the advice of human instructors; but when it comes to the matter of how each one of us should abide in Christ, of how we should individually reflect his beauty, our final mentor must be the Holy Spirit himself.

We have seen what true holiness is *not;* let us now see what

HOLINESS IS

Holiness is a way of life based, not on external rules, but on internal motivation. It arises from *a life-principle planted in us by God*. It is not a creed, but a MAN - Christ himself. It is not a struggle to be good, but simply living out the imparted life of Christ.

Holiness is positive, not negative; it is an affirmation, not a denial. It consists, not of prohibitions, but of opportunities. It is not something you *get*, it is something you already *have*. But although you have it, it must be worked out by faith, through knowledge of the word of God, and in co-operation with the Holy Spirit.

Those joyful ideas now entice us -

SANCTIFIED BY FAITH

It is vital to begin here, with faith.

Before you can ever become holy in *practice* you must reckon yourself to be holy in *principle*. Like every other spiritual blessing, holiness must be received by *faith* before it can be realised in *fact*. The law of Christ applies here as it does everywhere: *"believe that you receive, and you will receive"* (Mk 11:24). You must accept that you are *already* holy before you can actually *appear* holy. You can do well only after you are made well by the grace of God in Christ.

The work begins with him, not with us.

Holiness then, is *not* a standard we are striving to achieve; rather, it is a gift we are called on to receive, a promise we are challenged to believe.

Now that does not mean there will be no conflict in your pursuit of holiness. There will be. But it should not be a fight of the flesh, but of faith: *"Fight the good fight of faith; take hold of the eternal life to which you were called"* (1 Ti 6:12).

In this matter of faith, *sanctification* follows the same pattern as *justification* -

> ➢ to be *justified*, three things are necessary -
> 1. to hear the gospel of salvation
> 2. to believe in the promise of God

3. to yield to the regenerative work of the Holy Spirit.

➤ to be *sanctified* three things are necessary -
   1. to hear the gospel of holiness
   2. to believe in the promise of God
   3. to yield to the sanctifying work of the Holy Spirit.

Thus, just as you were justified only as a result of faith; so you will be sanctified only as a result of faith (Ac 15:9; 26:18; Ro 1:17). But since faith itself is ultimately a gift of God, all the glory of your sanctification belongs to him, along with the glory of your salvation.

So it is finally all of grace. We cannot be *saved* by works, neither can we be *sanctified* by works. Only those works that spring from faith in the promise of God and in his enabling grace are acceptable to the Lord (Ga 3:1-3), for the praise for such works belongs only to him. But any work offered to God as the price of pardon, or to build a self-made sanctity, will be instantly swept away.

It is apparent then that we grow in sanctification only as we first increase in faith, and then, by faith, appropriate the means God has made available to enable us to go on into holiness.

That brings me to the next question: *"What are the means by which I can go on to live righteously?"*

THE MEANS OF SANCTIFICATION

To aid you in sanctifying yourself and in maintaining your vow of separation, the grace of God has made available several mighty weapons. Diligent and faithful use of these weapons will ensure success. Among them are

➤ the fear of God (2 Co 7:1)
➤ love of the brethren (1 Th 3:12-13)
➤ prayer (1 Th 5:23; Lu 18:1)
➤ the blood of Christ (He 10:29; 13:12; 1 Jn 1:8-2:2)
➤ the word of God (Jn 17:17, 19; Ep 5:26; 1 Ti 4:5; 2 Pe 1:3-4)
➤ walking in the Spirit.

The last one is probably the chief means of practical sanctification. Once God has secured our active and intelligent co-operation in the pursuit of holiness, he is then able to set in motion his own grace, which will make that holiness real in daily life. But this grace is communicated to us especially through the influence and power of the indwelling Spirit. Only to people empowered by the Holy Spirit could Paul write, *"Walk in the Spirit and you will not fulfil the lusts of the flesh"* (Ga 5:16, A.V. See also 1 Co 6:19-20; 2 Co 3:18; Ez 36:27).

Since the ministry of the Spirit is the chief means of our daily sanctification, it deserves a separate section -

THE MINISTRY OF THE SPIRIT

As I have already shown, through the new birth and water baptism we became identified with the Lord Jesus Christ in his death, burial, and resurrection. But that is basically a *legal* identification. Having believed in Christ we gain a *legal* right to all of the blessings of salvation.

But while the new birth gave you access to all of the promises of God it did not automatically bring any *realisation* of those promises.

See *Romans 8:9-10*. In that crucial passage Paul teaches

> - that life came to you when you believed in the Lord Jesus Christ;
> - to that extent you possess the grace of God and are indwelt by the Spirit of Christ;
> - yet you soon find that your mortal body is still *"dead"* because of the sin that lies in it.
> - but, having been *born* of the Spirit and quickened *spiritually*, if we are then *baptised* in the Spirit, we shall also be quickened *physically*.
> - so Paul says in the next verse (Ro 8:11), that God will *"give life to your mortal bodies also through his Spirit which dwells in you."*

Hence the apostle is saying, if you want to experience in your everyday life the fulness of God and the victory of Christ, *you should be filled with the Spirit.* Holy Spirit baptism is a vital key to holy living.

But even if you *are* filled with the Spirit, you may *still* find yourself bound by the lust of the flesh unless you also *"walk in the Spirit"*. For after declaring that God will quicken our mortal bodies by his indwelling Spirit, Paul qualified his statement by urging his readers to go on *to live by the Spirit* (Ro 8:12-14). That is because there are many Spirit-filled Christians who are not yet allowing the Holy Spirit to lead them, they are not truly walking in the Spirit, so they have not yet experienced the wealth, the privileges, the authority, the revelation, the strength, the satisfaction, that only the living sons of God can know.

So remember Paul's emphatic word: *"Walk in the Spirit and <u>you will not fulfil</u> the passions of the flesh."* And again, *"If you have discovered life through the Spirit, <u>then walk in the Spirit</u>* (Ga 5:16,25).

I want to show you now what it means to walk in the Spirit.

THE FLESH AND THE SPIRIT

See *Galatians 5:17*. In every Christian there is a struggle between the flesh and the Spirit. The grace of God within us holds us back from evil; but the evil within us holds us back from the grace of God. It is a struggle between the diminishing remains of sin, and the increasing grace of God.

The *"flesh"* (characterised in the Bible as *"the old nature"*) and the Spirit (*"the new nature"*, Ep 4:22-24) are always contrary to each other. The struggle between them will continue until life ends, or until Christ comes - for only then will *"this mortal become immortal and this corruptible become incorruptible"* (1 Co 15:53; Ph 3:20-21). Since this is so, you should not try to hide the existence of this conflict, as though it were something to be ashamed of, or as though it meant that you were not a true Christian. It is not something for which you should hate or condemn yourself. It is part of what Paul calls *"the good fight of faith"*.

However, though we cannot escape this conflict, it is eased by the fact that we may so walk before the Lord that whereas the flesh was one time utterly victorious, the Spirit now steadily assumes the ascendancy, so that we become *"more than conquerors"* in Christ (Ga 5:16; Ro 8:37).

What exactly is meant by the *"flesh"* and by the *"Spirit"*?

The influence of the flesh, and of the Spirit, is shown by the things they each produce. For the *"flesh"* see Ga 5:19-21. For the Spirit see Ga 5:22-23. A life that is pressing on into sanctification will see a cessation of fleshly works, and an increase in spiritual fruit.

WALK IN THE SPIRIT

If you walk in the Spirit you will not fulfil the works of the flesh. Yet even so, the flesh, lusting against the Spirit, will sometimes prevent you from being all that you want to be, and from doing all that you want to do. But though you may at times fail to do the things that you should, so long as you would do them if you could, and so long as you are striving to be led by the Spirit and to walk worthy of the Lord, you are not under the law (Ga 5:23b,18), and the mercy of God will provide pardon for your failures.

Nevertheless, we are all expected to allow the Spirit to lead us so that the victory of Christ will become more and more apparent in our lives. The lust of the flesh, in one way or another, may be with us until the day we die, but we are not obliged to yield to it, nor will we, if we walk in the Spirit.

So never be reconciled to defeat, never tolerate sin, never yield to despair, never be indifferent to failure!

We are obliged to renounce sternly any sin as soon as it reveals itself, and with all diligence to uproot it and cast it away. Even more, realising that there are hidden tendencies to evil within us, and all manner of sin that has not yet been discovered (Ro 3:10-18; Je 17:9; Mk 7:21-23) we are by every means at our disposal to search out and purge ourselves so that we may be fully conformed to the image of Christ (1 Th 4:1-4; 2 Ti 2:19-22).

PROGRESSIVE VICTORY

In the conflict between the flesh and the Spirit, the Spirit enables us to conquer progressively all evil and to continually appropriate more of the grace of Christ -

> *Do you not know that to be a friend of the world is to be an enemy of God? Do you suppose you can seek the friendship of the world without becoming hostile to God? Or do you imagine that the scripture is speaking to no purpose when it says, "The Spirit whom God has caused to dwell in us yearns over us with a jealous love"? But he gives more and more grace (through the*

> *power of the Holy Spirit) to overcome fully every evil tendency* (Ja 4:4-6, *paraphrased.)*

See also Ro 8:13-14; Ga 5:24. The latter reference speaks about the crucifixion of the flesh, with all its passions and desires. Crucifixion is a slow, lingering death. A crucified man does not die at once; but he is as good as dead, and every hour brings him nearer to death. So with us - every day should see both the death of some evil in our lives, and the approaching death of other sins and ungodly tendencies.

In every genuine believer, righteousness should be waxing ever stronger, while evil wanes ever weaker. Our experience should reflect in miniature the scripture which says:

> *There was a long war between the partisans of Saul and those of David; and David grew steadily stronger, while Saul became steadily weaker* (2 Sa 3:1).

ENTIRE SANCTIFICATION

There are various teachings which hold that a person, in this life, may become *"free of all sin"*, or at least *"free of all known sin"*. This teaching is sometimes called *"entire sanctification"*, or *"sinless perfection"*. Under its banner Christians are exhorted to strive for a place of faith where they will be perfectly free from sin; and they are often taught that this perfection can be gained in a moment of time, through an experience as definite as the new birth.

In a more modified form, the teaching holds that *"no Christian need knowingly or wilfully sin,"* and that, so long as we live according to the light we possess, we are counted as being without sin. In that state, God requires only that we do the best we can. The corruption and temptation that we still sense within us (it is said) are not reckoned to be sin.

I respect those who hold such views, and recognise their sincerity, and their desire to live before the Lord in perfect holiness. Yet I must reject this *"perfectionist"* view on the following grounds -.

(1) In effect, this teaching reduces the law of God to human capacity, it equates God's standard with our ability. But such an attitude must tend to remove any real incentive to strive for greater heights. And it is also manifestly unjust. In commercial life we are expected to repay the whole of our debts; chaos

would soon result if we were permitted to repay only as much as we felt we could afford! Yet that is the position of the relative perfectionist when he claims that God grades his law down to the moral condition of the Christian.

On the contrary, the Bible plainly shows that all coming short of the glory of God is sin (cp. Ro 3:23). So long as we fail in any particular to fulfil the perfect character and holiness of Christ and to display the full beauty of the nine-fold fruit of the Spirit, to that extent the works of the flesh have striven successfully against the Spirit and we are guilty of sin. Every time we fail in our desire to be like Jesus in word and deed the flesh has lusted against the Spirit, has shown itself contrary to the Spirit, and has conquered.

Does that mean we shall never be like Christ? Not by any means! Does it mean that we can excuse failure? Not for a moment! But recognising the infirmity that is within us, we are driven to an entire dependency upon the grace of God, and to a fervent walk in the Spirit, for only thus may we crucify the flesh and steadily bring forth the character of Christ.

The scripture teaches us that we should not sin; but it also says, if we do sin, we have an Advocate with the Father (1 Jn 2:1-2).

(2) The perfectionist theory, as well as having an inadequate conception of the law of God, has a limited view of sin. It claims that sin consists only of voluntary transgression, whereas surely sin is found in any thought, impulse, desire, or emotion that is not conformed to God's will (Ja 1:13-15).

The perfectionist claims that involuntary sin, that is, sin committed without deliberation or the assent of the will, is not sin. But again, it must be obvious that all coming short of God's law is sin. The demand of God is perfection; and not perfection such as we can ourselves achieve, but divine perfection - see Mt 5:48; 1 Pe 1:15-16.

(3) In claiming the possibility of perfect freedom from sin, the perfectionist must also claim that a person is perfectly able at any time to obey the whole law of God. But that ignores the obvious fluctuations of human affections and human dispositions; it denies the influence of habits and character formed across years of sinful living; and it credits a person with

the strength of will and clarity of understanding possessed by Jesus.

Can it really be supposed that we always know what is right and always have the power and will to choose what is right? Is it really scriptural to say that if we do the wrong thing because we do not know the right thing, we are not guilty of sin?

Surely the plain statements of scripture show that we are obliged to keep the whole law of God, and nothing less than the whole law (Ja 2:10). The law is a glorious unity, not a mass of separate ordinances; thus he who violates one point of the holiness of God becomes guilty of the whole. Even when men knew nothing of the law of God, they were still accounted guilty (Ro 5:14).

Other scriptures teach us that the ability to choose what is right and to do it is something we gain only through long fellowship with Christ, yet still not fully until Jesus comes (He 5:14; Ph 2:12-16; 1 Co 13:12; Cl 1:9-10.)

> (4) The Bible refutes the idea that anyone can live on the earth without sin - (1 Kg 8:46; Ec 7:20; Ja 3:2). Confession of hidden sin has been made by the finest saints. In fact, it is usually true that the closer a soul comes to Christ, and the more it advances in holiness, the more conscious of sin does that soul become, the more it shrinks from claiming that holiness has already been attained, and the more strongly it recognises its need of sanctification - (Ph 3:12-14; 1 Co 4:4-5; Jb 9:20).
>
> (5) Ultimate perfection, entire sanctification, will be realised in each believer only in the day of resurrection - Ph 3:20-21; Cl 3:4; 1 Jn 3:2; Ju 24-25.

A scriptural attitude would appear to be

- ➢ always strive for perfection, expecting to overcome sin, but never claim to be perfect nor to have fully overcome.
- ➢ to claim perfection savours of pride, and seems to betray ignorance of the corruption of the human heart and of the extent and purpose of the law of God.
- ➢ a right understanding of the scope of the law will put a quick end to any claim of personal perfection. As David said, *"I have seen*

an end of all perfection, for thy commandment is exceeding broad" (Ps 110:96, KJV).

➢ we can never excuse sin, nor in any way tolerate it, for we must always press toward the likeness of Christ. Having righteousness imputed to us in Christ, we cannot help but strive to reflect that righteousness in daily practice.

➢ so, knowing that without holiness we shall never see the Lord, let us ever pursue it with zeal, knowing that in the end all righteousness comes to us not by our own effort, but by faith in the finished work of Christ, and by the continuing ministry of the Holy Spirit.

ADDENDUM

Here is a group of additional references, which highlight the various things discussed in this chapter -

(1) dealing with faith as an agent of sanctification (Ro 6:11; 1 Pe 2:24; Cl 3:3; Ep 1:15-2:1; 3:14-19).

(2) References using the language of warfare for our contest with sin (Ro 6:13-14; Ep 6:10-18; He 12:4; 2 Ti 2:3-4; 2 Co 10:3-5; 1 Ti 6:12; 1 Pe 2:11).

(3) References using the language of athletics (1 Co 9:24-27; 1 Ti 2:5; He 12:1; Ph 2:13-14).

(4) References indicating that the flesh must be put to death (Ro 6:6; 7:4-6; Cl 3:5-6).

(5) References to the *"old nature"* versus the *"new nature"* (Ep 4:22-24; Cl 3:9-10; Ro. 13:14; 7:15-8:2).

All those references indicate a life-long process of eliminating sin and of growing in righteousness. All of them accept the reality and possibility of sin in the believer's life; but they all just as strongly, in fact more so, emphasise the victory that is available to those who take hold of the many weapons provided by God. By these weapons we are well able to face sin in any of its forms, and to overcome it. May God give you wisdom to recognise sin when it is present, and to know which spiritual resource you should use for victory -

> *Although we are just ordinary men we are not fighting an ordinary war, for the weapons we fight with are not those the world uses, but are supernaturally strong to destroy strongholds!* (2 Co 10:3-4).

CHAPTER SIX:

POSITION

One of the most helpful ideas you can grasp in relation to victorious Christian life is the difference between your *standing* and your *state*.

Your *standing* refers to your legal *position* with Christ in the heavenlies - that is, your present spiritual union with Christ in his resurrection, ascension, and enthronement at the Father's right hand.

Your *state* refers to your actual *condition* on earth - that is, the degree to which you have managed to appropriate the fulness of Christ in your daily life.

Paul's letters to the Ephesians and the Colossians are built around this theme. In each case, the first half of the letter is devoted to the believer's *standing* in Christ; and the second half deals with the believer's *state* on earth. But the same method can be observed in all of Paul's instructions to the various churches. Always he wanted them to know *who* they were in Christ before he told them *what* they should do as Christians. *Insight* must come before *action, revelation* before *requirement, doctrine* before *duty*.

How often that pattern is reversed! Time and again people are told that they must *do* holiness before they can pronounce themselves holy; or that they must *live* victoriously before they can declare themselves victors; or that they must *act* righteously before they can confess themselves righteous; and so on. But the end result of making personal *behaviour* the criterion of one's *position* before Christ is to lapse into suffocating *legalism*. Grace is abandoned. Law triumphs - with disastrous effects in the frustrated experience of God's people.

A concise example of the difference between *standing* and *state* can be found in *Colossians 3:1-5*, which declares (a) you are *already* glorified with Christ in the heavenlies; (b) this glory is not visible on earth; (c) until it becomes visible at the rapture, it must be appropriated by faith. The remainder of this chapter will explore various aspects of those themes.

YOUR STANDING AND YOUR STATE

YOUR STANDING

The scriptures declare that in Christ you are already:
- an heir of God (Cl 1:12)
- a citizen of heaven (1:13)
- redeemed (1:14)
- reconciled and perfect (1:21-22)
- indwelt by divine glory (1:27)
- complete (2:10)
- risen into the heavenlies (2:12)
- dead to the world (3:3)
- and so on.

All that, just from Colossians! You could find much more if you searched through the other NT letters.

Notice that each one of those blessings is true *now* of every Christian. They are not future promises but present provision. They belong to you *today*. They are yours simply because of your union with Christ through faith. They represent the heavenly status God has given you in Christ. This is how you appear *"in his sight"* (Cl 1:22). No matter how you appear in your own eyes, or in the eyes of the world, or of the devil, in *God's* eyes you are seen complete, perfect, righteous, and victorious in Christ.

The Father has resolved to see each of his children only as they appear in Christ. He never separates us from Christ. We are visible to him only through the image of Christ. In us the Father always beholds the beauty and holiness of his Son.

Notice: this status you have before the Father in heaven is all based on the work of Christ. It has nothing to do with your personal achievement. You can *add* nothing to this work of Christ, and you can *take* nothing from it. It is all a free gift of God's grace, granted to all who profess Christ as Lord.

But now comes a vital truth: *the believer's legal standing in the heavenlies in Christ does not automatically become the practice of daily life.*

In fact, a person's *actual* state on earth may be quite different from his *legal* standing in heaven. Though his *standing* may be one of righteousness, his *state* may be one of *un*righteousness. He may appear in heaven beautiful in holiness, but on earth ugly in wickedness.

How can that be? How long can God endure such a discrepancy? How can such a difference be reconciled? How can it be changed?

Before those questions can be answered we need to look at -

YOUR STATE

YOUR STANDING IS NOT AFFECTED BY YOUR STATE

Read Colossians 3:5-9 and Ephesians 4:17-22.

Would you be willing to call those people Christians? What wretched sins they were committing! How could Christian people ever be guilty of such rotten behaviour?

I know what many modern preachers would do if they found a congregation behaving like those people at Ephesus and Colossae. The preacher would assault those fallen saints with awful words of denunciation and doom. He would command the people to repent and purify their lives. Only after they had stopped sinning, the preacher would say, could those people justly claim to be Christians, holy, and enthroned with Christ.

Now, Paul too wanted the people to live righteously. He loathed sin. He never made any excuse for it nor indifferently permitted people to remain in it.

But neither did he put human action before divine grace.

Paul understood that the gospel is a four-letter word, "DONE," not a two-letter word, "DO." So, before he condemned their faults, he showed them the way of faith. He gave them revelation before he growled rebuke. He brought them inspiration before he delivered instruction. He set them in the heavenlies with Christ before he gave any attention to what was happening in the earthlies. Or, to sum it all: he gave them a heavenly <u>position</u> before he sought to change their earthly <u>condition</u>.

Two important ideas come out of this -

> (a) A poor state does not change a believer's standing. Although some of the people at Colossae, for example, were guilty of "fornication, impurity, passion, etc." (Cl 3:5-9), Paul still says they were "risen with Christ, and hidden with Christ in God" (vs. 1-4) - a statement almost impossible to believe if it were not found in scripture. Yet there is no equivocation in the apostle's language. Though there was much scarlet sin in the lives of those Colossians, Paul still unhesitatingly gave them the highest possible standing in Christ.

> (b) But having done that, the apostle then made their <u>unchanged</u> standing the basis of an appeal for a <u>changing</u> state. He wanted their earthly condition to reflect their heavenly position. He had no tolerance for sin. He was utterly committed to holiness. But he knew that people never get rid of sin by struggling against it. We gain victory only as we re-position ourselves in Christ, reckon upon ourselves God's new identity, and, from the vantage point of the throne, take authority over the flesh, Satan, and sin. All of which is a matter, not of will nor of work, but of faith.

POWERFUL BENEFITS ARISE FROM THIS PRINCIPLE

When you learn to assert your legal standing in Christ *before* you make any attempt to alter your actual state on earth, certain benefits follow -

> (a) You find yourself in a place of unbroken peace with God, for your relationship with the Father is no longer based upon your own merits, but solely upon the merits of Christ (Ro 5:1). Whether *your* performance is excellent or awful, you know that *Christ* perfectly pleased the Father *on your behalf*, and that all the joy the Father found in Christ he now finds in you. Indeed, you become so satisfied with the perfections of Christ (now attributed to you by the Father's grace), you scorn all thought of presenting any worth of your own as a basis for communion with God. Grasping the righteousness of Christ in *"your right hand and in your left"* (so that there is no room for any self-wrought righteousness), you hold up that alone before the Father, knowing you are fully accepted in the Beloved (2 Co 6:7b; Ep 1:6).

No greater welcome can ever be given than comes to you through your union with Christ!

> (b) You escape the feeling that you must *"work your way back"* into God's favour after you have committed some sin. Have you not often felt just that way? Having done something *wrong*, there is a feeling you must now, before you can be welcome in God's presence, do several things that are *right*! You feel alienated from God. You feel distant from the throne. Surely, before you dare to approach the Holy One, you must perform some compensating labor of righteousness?

But how can that be? How can you *"work your way back"* to God when you are *already* standing there in heaven, before the throne, in his presence, highly favoured by the Father for Christ's sake?

> (c) You gain an unbroken right to speak and act in the authority of Christ; which then becomes the only viable way to destroy sin and to live righteously. Sin cannot rob you of that right. It has been bestowed upon you by the Father because of what Christ wrought on your behalf. The Father needs no further incentive. You cannot improve upon the work of Christ. Nothing you can do will make him more willing than he is already to grant you full authority over Satan and sin.

You cannot earn the Father's benediction of righteousness by struggling to live righteously. Indeed, you will *become* righteous only when you boldly declare that you *are* righteous. The heavenly reality must precede the earthly. There is no other way that is acceptable to God. Why? Because anything else is a work of the flesh, an act of self-righteousness, full of law, empty of grace, and disgusting to God (Ro 10:4; 3:21-22, 27-28).

Does this leave us free to sin with impunity?

Of course not. The purpose of God is always to rid us, not merely of sin's *guilt*, but also of its *grip*. Who could be content to be holy in the reckoning of God in heaven without also desiring to live holy before God on earth?

That takes us on to the third principle -

NARROWING THE GAP
KNOWING AND DOING

It is now plain that Christian life is primarily a matter of narrowing the gap between our unchanging *standing* and our constantly changing *state*. The true Christian will be always striving to work out in daily life what is constantly true of him in heaven.

Are you holy in heaven? Then you will want to be holy on earth!

Has God pronounced you righteous in Christ? Then you will want to be righteous in life!

Have you been given in heaven invincible authority over all of the power of Satan? Then you will want to exercise that dominion on earth!

There is no other allowable purpose for discovering what God has done for us in Christ in the heavenlies than to make that divine glory a reality in daily life. But we must first *know* before we can *do*. *"<u>Know</u> the truth,"* said Jesus, *"and the truth will set you free!"* (Jn 8:32). Undeniably, those who truly *know* will also *do*. Nothing less can satisfy them. Those who have no heart to *do* simply show they have never truly *known*.

ONLY FOR THOSE WHO ARE IN CHRIST

We must enter with goodwill into this process of *"narrowing the gap"* - that is, of striving by faith to bring into our daily experience what is true of us in Christ.

There are two inescapable reasons for this -

   (a) Continuation of your legal standing depends utterly upon continuation of your union with Christ. You have no righteous standing apart from Christ. If you are declared holy by God, it is only because you are *"in Christ."* But to continue *"in Christ"* means maintaining faith in Christ, for faith alone enables us to apprehend the grace of God, and to become the recipients of all that is contained in his great salvation.

   (b) But that faith, and that union with Christ, *cannot* be sustained in the presence of wilful, continual, and unrepented sin (Cl 3:6; Ep 5:3-7; He 10:26-31; etc.) Those who persist in unrighteousness, without shame, without sorrow, without any desire to change, will put faith to death, sear their own consciences, and be cut off from Christ. But if they no longer belong to Christ they no longer have any refuge in the heavenlies. They are fallen back into iniquity and face only the fearful wrath of God (He 6:4-6).

So it is finally impossible, in the vivid phrase of Jude, to *"pervert the grace of our God into licentiousness"* without also soon *"denying our only Master and Lord, Jesus Christ"* (vs. 4). But to deny that Jesus is Lord is to lose his grace and to merit hell in place of heaven.

Thus it is clear that knowing, believing, and confessing who you are in Christ in the heavenlies, is God's way to overcome sin and to live victoriously. And it is clear that this is a life-long process as day by day, through faith, we endeavour to *"narrow the gap."* But it is also clear that people who foolishly depend upon their heavenly standing, who make no attempt to bring their *state* into conformity with that *standing*, bring their very salvation into jeopardy.

God is not mocked. Anyone who continues to love sin will be enslaved by it and banished from the kingdom of God.

WHAT IF YOU SIN?

What effect then *does* sin have on your heavenly standing?

That depends, not upon the seriousness of the sin, whether it is great or small, but upon your attitude toward it, and the way you handle it.

If you are careless about sin, feeling no guilt, nor any compulsion to repent and be rid of it, then your state is perilous indeed.

But if your conscience is tender, if you tremble at any falling short of the glory of God, if you yearn for holiness to govern your every thought, word, and action, then you are close to the heart of God! In such a case, as soon as sin is recognised it should be followed by repentance, and then at once by a bold claim upon the pardon of God (1 Jn 1:9). That done, you should *straight away* re-affirm your *legal standing* in Christ, refusing to be bowed down by guilt or to wallow in self-pity.

You cannot pray, or work, or weep, or earn, or plead your way back to the throne of God. The fact is, you never left it! The mere occurrence of sin in a believer's life cannot disturb his or her position in Christ in the heavenlies. Your *standing* is not affected by your *state* - unless that state is one of deliberate, unrepentant, continuance in sin, which cuts the sinner away from Christ. But, aside from such a reprobate condition, you can be confident that the daily fluctuations of your *state* (from better to worse, and worse to better) do not change your *standing*. The moment you turn your face to God, and trust in the blood of the cross, that moment, you have *undelayed, unhindered access to all that belongs to you in the heavenlies in Christ.*

Tears, toils, torment, will not you give you a molecule more right to approach the throne of God than you can gain from simple faith in Christ (He 10:19-23).

THE MEANS OF GRACE

It is evident, then, that *"narrowing the gap"* is not a matter of legal restraints, nor of fierce struggle, nor of rugged determination, but of *trust in the promise of God*. But what is the source of that trust? It should be a natural product of using the means of grace that are available to us - such as meditation each day in scripture, believing prayer, encouraging fellowship, positive ministry, and the like. There can be no growth of genuine faith without the constant use of those provisions God has made for the nourishment of faith.

But beware! Take care to starve the hunger of the flesh to turn the means of divine grace into works of self-righteousness. So often, the very things God intended for life become instead a source of death. Your flesh is very adept at that kind of transformation.

For example: how easily people can turn Bible reading into a law of righteousness. They come to feel, if they have read their Bible today, and prayed, they will surely appear more righteous to God, and walk more firmly in his favour, than if they had forgotten to read or pray. But that is law, not grace; it will bring death, not life.

A time of daily devotion cannot give you any more righteous standing, nor make you any more eligible for divine favour, than already belongs to you freely in Christ. Many benefits may come to you from prayer, scripture, worship, giving, and the like, *but they do not include a more righteous standing, nor a greater claim upon the favour of God.* You are either fully righteous in Christ, or you have no righteousness at all. You either stand already in Christ before the throne of God, or you will *never* have access to that throne.

No work of yours, no matter how pious, or noble, or sacrificial, can in the slightest enhance the heavenly position you possess by virtue of your union with Christ.

FROM POSITION TO POSSESSION

The legal standing you have in Christ in the heavenlies, as we have seen, is intended to provide the basis upon which you boldly grasp the promises of God, tread down the devil, and live a richly abundant life in the favour of God.

That will not happen of its own accord.

Vigorous and steadfast faith is needed.

And also self-discipline.

Nothing in your legal standing removes from you the need to serve God daily with all your heart, to deny the flesh, to oppose the devil, and to fight the good fight of faith.

But there is a difference between doing those things from a standpoint of strength in contrast with one of weakness. There is an even greater difference between doing them, not as an effort to *earn* heaven's favour, but rather as an *expression* of what we know we already possess in the heavenlies.

Because I know God is already fully pleased with me in Christ I strive to live up to that grace-given status. But, by first positioning myself with Christ in the heavenlies, I can strive as one who is strong, not weak. In the heavenlies I have access to all the resources I need to accomplish fully the will of God.

Again, I serve the Lord, not to *become* righteous, but to express the glorious righteousness that is totally mine now in Christ. After all, I am already *"the righteousness of God in Christ."* What can I possibly add to that? What could possibly improve *God's own* righteousness, which is freely attributed to me in Christ? Would I insult the Father by suggesting that *his* righteousness is inadequate, that it needs an occasional dollop of mine?

God forbid!

I am content with Christ's provision.

But while I cannot work for the *favour* of God, I *can* work for his *reward*. There is an inheritance available to the saints in the coming kingdom of God, and we are urged many times in scripture to give ourselves to the quest of that heavenly prize.

There are two other vital uses you can make of your legal standing in Christ -

TO RESIST SATAN

You should use your legal standing with Christ in heaven as the sole basis upon which you resist Satan, whether he attacks you by word, thought, or deed (1 Co 10:3-5). Depend upon no other merit save that of Christ. Trust no other right save that conferred upon you by Christ. Use no other authority save that which you have in the name of Jesus. Nothing you can do can either add to, nor take from, the full dominion over satanic power God has given you in his Son.

Various spiritual exercises you can do (prayer, worship, Bible reading, fasting) may enhance your *understanding* of your heavenly possessions and quicken your *faith* in appropriating them - but the possessions themselves are as rich as they are ever going to be. No work of yours can either increase or diminish them.

Do everything you can to stir up faith. But in the process, keep reminding yourself that mastery over the devil belongs to you *only* because of who you *are* in Christ, so that Satan is obliged to yield to you *only* when you *act* in Christ.

TO APPROACH GOD

You should use your legal standing with Christ in heaven as the sole basis upon which you approach the throne of God in bold prayer (He 10:19-23). Away with all carnal conceit that you can build some edifice of personal righteousness, and thus become more acceptable to God than you are in Christ alone. The Father can give you no higher welcome to his presence than he gives you in Christ. Nothing can bring you nearer to the favour of God than you are brought by the righteousness of Christ. Breathe nothing of your own name nor anything of your own achievement. Speak only the name of Jesus. Let his merits be all your contentment and the source of all your boldness.

CONCLUSION

The main idea in this chapter has been simply this: in general, your standing is not affected by your state.

That becomes an important truth when it is remembered that none of us is entirely free from sin. In some respect, all of us are all the time coming short of the glory of God - either by the things we are doing, or the things we are not doing. Hence, if our standing in heaven depended upon our state on earth, none of us would ever have any position before the throne of God! Or, at best, our position would be endlessly changing. But now there is immense security in knowing that whatever fluctuations of faith and conduct may overtake our earthly situation, our legal standing in Christ remains steady.

But it must be emphasised again, this truth is not an encouragement to sin, it provides no licence for iniquity, although some have tried to treat it so (Ro 6:1-4).

On the contrary, knowledge of your secure heavenly standing should become at once your best incentive for overcoming sin, and your best method of overcoming it.

In the end, there are only two choices for changing yourself: (a) you can look ahead, set up an image of what you want to be, and struggle to achieve it; or (b) you can look up, see what you are in Christ, and begin the joyful task of realising that Christ-given potential.

An illustration. Suppose a young man becomes enamoured with the idea of being a great tenor. He begins singing lessons. His voice has a certain quality, but it soon becomes clear he will never rise above mediocrity as a singer. Even if he were to struggle for years, he will never possess the talent to fill a vast theatre with glorious song. If he is sensible, he will abandon his quest, and content himself with another career.

But if he were born with the innate gifts of a Caruso, he would know that music was already in him, he was already a world-class tenor. All that would then be required of him would be to bring out and perfect the gift he had received from heaven.

Now that task might cost him enormous labor, many sacrifices, years of training and practice. But what a difference between a man with the voice of a crow trying to become Caruso, and Caruso trying to become Caruso!

How do you teach a cat to bark? There is only one way. Turn him into a dog, and he will bark naturally! So God gives us a new identity in Christ, and then bids us go and live it out.

How do you make a sinner righteous? By hanging good works on him, like putting pears onto an orange tree, hoping to make it a pear tree? No! Make that sinner righteous inside, and he will soon begin to produce righteous fruit.

Let the lesson be learned.

You will never be any better than you know yourself to be now in the heavenlies in Christ. You are not what you think you are. You are not what others think you are. You are what God says you are. And by virtue of your standing in Christ, God says you are his own righteousness, blessed with every spiritual blessing in the heavenlies!

Accept the identity God has given you. Accept your position in Christ. Remain secure in your legal standing. And from that place of limitless advantage go out to fulfil the purpose of the Father for your life.

CHAPTER SEVEN:

LEGALISM

The Bible abounds with references to *"the law of God"*, which is said to be *"holy, just, good, and eternal."* In many places, people are solemnly commanded to keep God's law and heavy penalties are prescribed for its violation. But in other places, especially in the NT, the law is said to be *"ineffective, dead, obsolete"*, supplanted by the grace of God. Many people find it difficult to reconcile such contradictory statements. For example, what are you going to do with statements as opposite as these?

> *For the law is holy, and the commandment is holy and righteous and good* (Ro 7:12). But then the same apostle says: *(The law is) a covenant of death, carved in letters on stone, (which has now) faded away* (2 Co 3:7-11).

Or how about the contrast in these statements? -

> *Until heaven and earth pass away, not one comma, not a single dot, will pass away from the law until it has all been fulfilled. Whoever then abandons even the least of these commands, or teaches anyone else to do so, will be called least in the kingdom of heaven* (Mt 5:18-19) . . . *Nobody can be justified by the works of the law but only by faith in Christ Jesus . . . not by the works of the law, because by the works of the law no one can be justified* (Ga 2:16).

What then? Shall we keep the law? All of it? Part of it? None of it?

For people whose earnest desire is to please God, these are vital questions, and this chapter will attempt an answer to them.

WHAT IS MEANT BY THE LAW

The word *"law"* in the NT usually refers to the law Moses gave Israel at the time of the Exodus (cp. Jn 1:17). [25] This law is commonly divided into three major groups:

> ***The Commandments***, that is, the famous Ten Commandments, which provided the basis for Israel's moral law (Ex 20:1- 17).

> ***The Judgments*** or ***Statutes***, which governed Israel's social, commercial, and political life (Ex 21:1-23:33; De 12:1-26:19).

> ***The Ordinances***, which directed Israel's worship and religious life (Ex 25:1-31:18).

Those divisions are not absolute, there are exceptions, but they are helpful and broadly true, and they provide a basis upon which to decide whether or not the law of Moses is applicable to us -

THE JUDGMENTS

It is not difficult to decide the NT attitude toward the Judgments. Christ himself absolutely over-ruled some of them. For example, we find that the *eye for an eye* of Moses becomes the *turn the other cheek* of Christ (Mt 5:38-42; Ex 21:24). As a rule of life for Christians, the Judgments have been generally abolished.

That does not mean they have no value. They possess inestimable value, for they display the basic standards of justice and equity that govern the kingdom of God and upon which the legal codes of our Western civilisations have been built. Hence those ancient Mosaic judgments are still exercising a profound influence upon our society.

---

[25] Some exceptions are: (1) references that describe the entire OT as "the law" (Lu 5:17; 16:17; Jn 10:34; 12:34); (2) references that speak of "the law of Christ" - that is, the "principles" of the gospel (Ro 3:27; 8:2; 9:21; Ga 6:2; Ja 1:25; 2:8); (3) references that speak of "the law" (principle) of sin (Ro 7:21,23,25); (4) references that speak of gentile law (1 Co 6:1). This list is not complete; other references could be added to it, but not many, for most of the occurrences of "law" in both Testaments refer to the law of Moses.

Nonetheless, they do not comprise a standard by which Christians can measure their relationship with God. In many of their specific details they are no longer morally binding, nor relevant to human salvation. An example of this is found in the Food Laws, which rather surprisingly remain a matter for argument among some Christians -

THE FOOD LAWS

By *"Food Laws"* I mean the strictures Moses enforced against eating certain *"unclean"* foods. Are those foods still *"unclean"*? Many Christians think so, and firmly resolve to eat only the foods Moses pronounced *"clean"*. [26]

It is usually assumed by such people that the foods forbidden by the ancient law must be inherently bad to eat, and unhealthy. Yet there does not appear to be any firmly established reason for such a sweeping assertion. The reasons for calling some foods *"unclean"* may have been related to health in some instances; but mostly the prohibitions seem to have arisen out of (1) the social taboos of that time; (2) an idolatrous use of the forbidden foods by the surrounding nations; (3) a simple desire to establish a separate and unique identity for Israel (cp. circumcision).

Those who observe the food laws today are rather arbitrary in their choice of laws to obey. It is hardly reasonable to invest the food laws with special value while ignoring the multitudinous regulations Moses also gave about household duties, cooking, clothing, building, etc. No-one reckons all of *those* laws are binding on today's society. It seems illogical to isolate the food laws and to credit *them* with lasting value and obligation, but to ignore the remainder. If we are debtors to part of the law, then we are debtors to all of it!

The apostles were well aware of this, and in quite plain terms they released the church from any duty to keep these *"judgments"* (Ac 10:9-16; 15:5-29; Ro 14:1-3,14,17; 1 Co 8:6-8; Cl 2:14-23; 1 Ti 5:1-5; He 9:9,10; 13:9.)

Paul's opinion appears to have been that those who believe they should *"eat only vegetables"* are *"weak in the faith!"* Hardly an encouragement to become an observer of meats and drinks!

---

[26]   See Le 3:14-17; 7:22-27; 11:1-47; 22:8; De 14:3-21.

But if there is still doubt, surely this passage from the gospel is final:

> *Jesus said to them, 'How is it that you are so slow to understand? Do you not realise that anything that comes into you from the outside cannot defile you, since it enters, not your spirit but your stomach, and then passes on into the drain, and so goes away from you?"* (Thus he declared all foods clean.) (Mk 7:18-19).

Whether or not certain of the forbidden foods make a healthy diet is of little value as far as the Bible is concerned; that is a matter for dieticians to decide, not theologians. The Bible is concerned with moral and spiritual issues, not with things that are merely physical.

But there is a grave fault many fall into who keep the food laws, even if ostensibly for reasons of health alone: adherence to these laws becomes for them a moral issue, a matter of righteousness and unrighteousness. They now consider it a sin to eat certain things, and a sign of grace or purity not to eat them. Such an attitude directly opposes the forthright teaching of Christ and the apostles. If a person feels God cannot answer his prayers because he has eaten a piece of pork, then he has moved away from the freedom of the gospel into the fetters of the old law. He has fallen from grace into legalism, from the liberty of the gospel into law's pitiful bondage.

THE ORDINANCES

The ordinances dealt with the different services, sacrifices, and offerings that belonged to the sanctuary. They governed the appointment of the priests and all the details of the worship of the people.

The letter to the *Hebrews* makes it clear that these ancient rites have no demands to make on the Christian. For us the ordinances of Israel have been completely annulled. We have in Christ a high priest whose ministry does not cease (thus doing away with the old priesthood), whose sacrifice of himself is once for all (thus doing away with the former many sacrifices), and whose temple is of God's building, not man's (thus doing away with the need for Israel's stone temple) (see He 7:24-28; 8:1-2; etc).

There remains only to consider -

THE COMMANDMENTS

In the Ten Commandments there are statements that are obviously relevant to us: "You shall have no other gods beside me;" "You shall not kill;" "You shall not steal;" "Honour your father and your mother;" etc.

Are these to be ignored in the same way as the judgments and ordinances? The answer to this question depends on where you find these injunctions. If you are thinking of them only in their original setting, that is, as one of the Ten Commandments given to Moses on Mt. Sinai, and engraved by God on stone, then the Bible implacably calls them a *"dispensation of death!"* In that form they have been forever cancelled out by Christ, being repealed in their entirety and replaced by a new body of statutes. An abrogated law is no longer valid. We are bound to observe only the current law.

Paul expounds this idea in his discussion on . . .

THE LETTER AND THE SPIRIT

See *2 Corinthians 3:6-18*. Don't fail to read that passage, for it is vitally important to a proper understanding of the relationship between the law and the gospel. It is also exciting reading!

The old version of this passage draws a contrast between *"the letter"* and *"the spirit"* - it reads,

> *(God) hath made us able ministers of the new testament; not of the letter, but of the spirit; for the letter killeth, but the spirit giveth life* (vs. 6. KJV).

People often misconstrue this to mean, *"We should observe the spirit of the law rather than the letter of the law."* But that is not the point. Note that Paul did not say, *"The letter of the law,"* but simply, *"the letter."* He was not talking about the surface meaning of the law in contrast with its deeper meaning (the *"spirit"*). By *"letter"* Paul meant *the law itself*, in its totality, as opposed to *the gospel*, which he calls *the spirit*.

The *"letter,"* therefore, is the old covenant given through Moses; the *"spirit"* is the new covenant given through Christ. If you read the whole passage again you will see that no other interpretation is possible.

In that one word *"letter"* (called by the RSV *"the written code,"*) Paul sums up all the commandments, ordinances, statutes, and regulations of ancient Israel. And to that list we must also add those additional standards men have written down for themselves - taboos about eating, drinking, clothing, pleasures, etc. Not being content with the ponderous list of Mosaic laws, they have superimposed this further pile of their own invention onto Israel's observances. All such rules are comprehended by Paul in the expression *"letter."*

Now Paul says two major things about this *"letter,"* this *"written code"*: it contains glory; its glory has been supplanted by the greater glory of the gospel. Then he explains why people cling to the old glory instead of grasping the new. Let us examine these ideas -

THE GLORY OF THE LAW

Nobody can doubt the glory of the ancient law of Moses. It was given to the great leader by God himself, amid scenes of terrifying majesty and splendour (Ex 19:10-25; 20:18-21; He 12:18-21). Paul emphatically asserts this glory

- ➢ (the law) carved in letters on stone came with splendour (vs. 7).
- ➢ there was splendour in the dispensation of (the law) (vs. 9).
- ➢ (the law) has splendour (vs. 10).
- ➢ (the law) came with splendour (vs. 11).
- ➢ in fact, so great was the glory of the law, *"the Israelites could not look at Moses' face because of its radiant splendour"* (vs. 7; and cp. Ex 34:29-30, 33-35).

Now, that glory still remains in the law, and those who keep the law experience its glory. Hence, you find people who talk about the great blessing they gain from keeping the sabbath (especially on Saturday); while others might speak of the benefits of keeping the food laws, or of observing any of the hundreds of commandments given by Moses.

Then there are those who do not emphasise the Mosaic statutes, but (as I have said) make lists of their own, dealing with clothing, jewellery, personal appearance, pleasures, times of devotion, entertainment, literature, music, culture, religious observances, and so on. When they succeed in keeping these self-imposed *"do's"* and *"dont's"* they feel holy; if they break them, they feel unholy. And they pass the same judgment on others.

But Paul dismisses them all:

> *Why do you submit to regulations like "Do not handle, Do not taste, Do not touch"? Such rules are all man-made, they are doctrines invented by men, they refer to things that will all perish as they are used. Admittedly, your rules may seem to be wise, for they do require deep devotion, self-abasement, and severe discipline of the body. But don't you realise that they have no value when it comes to conquering your evil thoughts and desires. In fact, they actually indulge the flesh because they foster spiritual pride* (Cl 2:20-23, paraphrased.)

However, despite that apostolic indictment, the *"letter"* continues to fascinate many people; they taste its glory and enjoy it, but sadly fail to discover -.

THE GREATER GLORY OF THE GOSPEL

Paul repeatedly draws an annihilating comparison between the law and the gospel

- ➢ the *law* is the letter that kills, but the *gospel* is the spirit that brings life (vs. 6).
- ➢ the *law* is the old covenant, the *gospel* is the new covenant, and we should proclaim the new, not the old (vs. 6).
- ➢ the *law* was carved on letters on stone, the *gospel* is imprinted on the *"tablets of human hearts"* (vs. 3,7).
- ➢ the *law* was the dispensation of death, the *gospel* is the dispensation of the Spirit (vs. 7).
- ➢ the glory of the *law* has faded away, the splendour of the *gospel* is eternal (vs. 7).
- ➢ the *law* was the dispensation of condemnation, the *gospel* is the dispensation of righteousness (vs. 9).
- ➢ the *law* once had splendour, the *gospel* has a splendour that surpasses it (vs. 10).

- the *law* was temporary, the *gospel* is permanent (vs. 11).
- the *law* is a cold letter, unmerciful, unyielding, impotent to change its adherents, destroying all who live by it; the *gospel* is a Man, warm, compassionate, merciful, able to give life.
- the *law* means fear and bondage; the *gospel* means faith and liberty.
- the *law* had *"splendour,"* the *gospel* has a splendour that is *"greater . . . (that) far exceeds . . . that surpasses . . . (that is) much more (splendid)."*
- in the words of the old version, the *law* is *"done away,"* but the glorious gospel *"remaineth"* (vs. 11).

Since these things are so, why do people still live by the law? Why, when they are freely offered a far greater, do they cling to the lesser glory? It is because

THEIR EYES ARE VEILED

When Moses came down from the mount he veiled his face (vs. 13). He did this, not to protect the people's eyes from the shining glory, *but to prevent them from witnessing the fading of that glory*!

Moses knew the radiance would soon fade, and he feared if the people saw it fading they would think God was no longer with him, and they would no longer respect the law. So he covered his face, and from that time on *removed the veil only when he entered the presence of the Lord* (Ex 34:34). He wore that veil until the end of his life, so that Israel never realised that the glory had faded. Not even Moses' death revealed the truth, for the people were unable to discover his body (De 34:6).

Figuratively speaking, that veil still covers the minds of many people, so they believe there is still glory in keeping the law (vs. 14-15). But Paul urges us to tear the veil away, see that the glory has gone out of the law, turn wholly to Christ, and so find perfect liberty (vs. 16-17).

Now there is a group of people whose eyes are still firmly veiled, who are persuaded there is still glory in the law: the people who cling to the fourth commandment, who claim it is mandatory for Christians to observe the sabbath -.

THE FOURTH COMMANDMENT

THE LAW IS HELPLESS

Shall we keep the sabbath? Or, for that matter, shall we keep any of the Ten Commandments as they are written in the OT, adhering to the terms and provisions that surround them there? If we can solve the problem in relation to the fourth commandment it is solved for them all.

Those who claim we must observe the old sabbath, put forward scores of scriptures that urge the solemnity, the sanctity, of the sabbath, and that stress the vast importance of keeping the sabbath day holy unto the Lord. But out of all their proof texts, the foundational one is *Exodus 20:8-10* (and cp. Ge 2:1-3). An examination of that passage shows that

(1) The sabbath has its roots in remotest antiquity. Nevertheless, until the giving of the law of Moses the Bible does not record any command given to any man to keep the sabbath. Indications are that the original custom was built simply on the basis of resting one day in seven. No doubt that is still wise; it is certainly pleasant; but, as we shall see, it is by no means morally binding on Christians.

(2) A command was given in the days of Moses, the Sabbath was legalised, and incorporated into the statutes that governed Israel's national, moral, and religious life.

Now, the custom observed by ancient peoples before the time of Moses, of keeping one day in seven, and even the example of the Lord God who rested on the seventh day, do not in themselves establish for us an obligatory law. But are we perhaps placed under obedience by the fact of the Sabbath law being included in the Ten Commandments?

(3) Some Christians maintain that the Ten Commandments have been abolished, all of them, so that we should now adhere only to those commandments that have been re-written into the New Covenant.

Others claim that we are solemnly bound by God, as Israel was, to keep the Ten Commandments. To them, the ancient law has never been repealed; it is still valid, and obligatory for all men, including the church. They seek to prove their case in this way:

- they divide the Law of Moses into two groups, *"ceremonial"* and *"moral"*
- the *"moral law"* is the Ten Commandments; all that remains is classed as *"ceremonial law"*
- they then claim that while Christ, at Calvary, abolished the *"ceremonial law,"* our ultimate salvation remains dependent upon us keeping the *"moral law,"* which includes the fourth commandment: *"keep the sabbath day holy."*

However, that we are not obliged to keep the *"moral law,"* as a condition *of salvation*, is evident from

> (a) The *"ceremonial law"* was given for one reason only, to *atone for transgression of the Ten Commandments*. Men and women could fully keep the *"ceremonial law"* and be blameless in its observance (Ph 3:6); but no man save Christ has ever yet succeeded in keeping the *"moral law."*
>
> (b) That it was this *"moral law,"* or the Ten Commandments, Christ perfectly fulfilled on our behalf (thereby removing the need for us to fulfil it), is evident in the following passages -

> *If the law had not spoken, I would never have known sin. For example, I would never have known what lust is if the law had not said, "You shall not lust!" Without from the law, sin remains dead . . . but when the commandment came, sin came alive and I died. The very commandment that should have made me alive instead brought death upon me* (Ro 7:7-10).

There we discover that the Ten Commandments, far from bringing forth salvation or making us acceptable to God served only to bring us under condemnation of sin, with its penalty of death. If we are to keep the law, then, and escape its punishment, we must keep it in the person of another, and that one is Christ -

> *For God has done what the law, weakened by our sinful nature, could never do. By sending his own Son in the likeness of sinful men and women, and to deal with sin, he has condemned all the sin that we do. His purpose was that everything the law commands may now be fulfilled in us, who no longer follow the dictates of our*

> *sinful natures, but instead yield to the Spirit. This means that the righteousness of God has been brought to light independently of the law (although both the law and the prophets bear witness to it), and this is the righteousness of God that comes through faith in Jesus Christ to all who believe. For we insist a person is justified by faith apart from any practice of the law, and through Christ everyone who believes can be freed from everything from which they could not be freed by the law of Moses. So on one hand, the earlier commandment is dismissed because of its weakness and uselessness (for the law made nothing perfect); on the other hand, a better hope is introduced through which we draw near to God* (Ro 8:3,4; 3:21-22,28; Ac 13:38,39; He 7:19).

In each one of those references the apostle highlights the helplessness of the law; he reinforces the indictment presented in the passage we have already considered (2 Co 3:6-18), that the law is a dead letter, whereas the gospel is a living spirit. No wonder he says in the same place that God had made him a minister of the new covenant (*"the spirit"*) not of the old (*"the letter"*). *"I preach the gospel of Christ,"* he is saying, *"not the law of Moses."*

Like Paul, I too say that God has not sent me to preach the Ten Commandments but to proclaim life and liberty through Christ.

> (c) There can be no evasion of the clear statement that those who hope to find salvation by keeping the Ten Commandments will find instead *death*. That written code *"kills;"* it is a ministry of *"death,"* and of condemnation.*" Against this backdrop of despair, Paul displays the beauty of the gospel*

- ➢ the *commandments* are cold letters; but the *gospel* is full of spirit and life.

- ➢ the *commandments* were mechanically engraved on stone; but the *gospel* is a seed planted in our hearts.

- ➢ the *commandments* have no feeling, no mercy, they are hard and implacable, leading only to condemnation; but the *gospel* is a Saviour, full of love and compassion.

- the *commandments* are impotent, they cannot help us, they have no transforming power; but the *gospel* is able to lift us into "the likeness of Christ, from one degree of glory to another."
- the *commandments* mean fear, bondage, and eternal death, but the *gospel* brings faith, liberty, and eternal life!

(4) It is therefore impossible to draw any nearer to God by the keeping of any law, including the Ten Commandments; to attempt to do so is to insult the full sufficiency of Christ's sacrifice and perfect obedience on our behalf. The scriptures unequivocally declare, that in our name and in our stead, Christ kept every provision of the law, so that we, in his name, may count ourselves to have fulfilled already its every requirement (Ro 5:19).

(5) It should now be evident that the Ten Commandments, for the Christian, belong to an obsolete code, they have been repealed; in their ancient form they have no power over us, we are not obliged to keep them.

Does that mean we are now free to steal, kill, lie, worship idols, be immoral, and so on? Of course not, because we are subject to a new law, the law of Christ. The law appertaining to the old covenant has been for us revoked; but we now owe obedience to the law of the new covenant.

As it happens, the new covenant includes many of the regulations that belonged to the old, including all of the Ten Commandments except one, and that exception is the fourth commandment. The new covenant embraces all the commandments but this: the NT nowhere obliges the church to keep the sabbath. The other nine commandments are all re-instated, in a new form, but the fourth commandment is omitted, yet not altogether, for it has been replaced by a different kind of sabbath-keeping -.

FROM THE OLD SABBATH TO THE NEW

(1) The NT does more than just omit the fourth commandment; it categorically declares that all of the old sabbath regulations have been repealed (Cl 2:16-17; Ga 4:10-11; Ro 13:5). Sabbatarians look at those passages in two different ways -

(a) There are some who say that the *"sabbath days"* mentioned by Paul are the *special* days of celebration observed by

Israel, which must be distinguished from the sacred *weekly* sabbath. The weekly sabbath held a unique place as part of the *"moral"* law, while all of the other sabbaths (the new moon festivals, harvest celebrations, religious convocations, etc.) belonged to the *"ceremonial"* law. The latter have been abolished, but the former remains. Therefore, it is said, while it is true that we no longer have to observe the special sabbaths, keeping the weekly sabbath remains mandatory for all true Christians.

However, there is not the slightest indication that the NT writers made such a distinction between the two groups of sabbaths. If Paul intended his dismissal of the sabbaths to be applied only to the secondary festivals, but not to the weekly sabbaths, then he was singularly careless in the way he expressed himself. Remember that he was writing to Gentile Christians, who would not be aware of the finer distinctions in the Jewish law.

It seems far more probable that the Colossians (for example) would take him to mean that they should discard all of the Jewish apparatus when he wrote: *"Let no one pass judgment on you . . . with regard to a festival or a new moon or a sabbath"* (2:16).

> (b) It is claimed also that worship on a day other than the Jewish sabbath (that is, on a day other than the seventh day of the week) was instituted by pagan leaders of the church after it had fallen into corruption and worldliness. Indeed, seventh-day sabbatarians argue that worship on Sunday (the first day of the week) was not instituted until the 4th century.

Is that a true claim?

Hardly. Even a casual look at church history will show that the following church fathers, along with many others, all testify that within a generation of the death of John, observance of *Sunday* (the *first* day of the week) was widespread among the early Christians - [27]

Barnabas (AD 100); Justin Martyr (AD 145), for whom the Sunday service was standard; Irenaeus (AD 155); Tertullian (AD 200); Eusebius (AD 315).

Melito of Sardis (AD 170) wrote a thesis on Sunday as *"the Lord's day."* The Didache (written c. AD 200) talks about Sunday as *"the Lord's day."* And Ignatius (AD 107) wrote in his Epistle to the Magnesians (8,9,10):

> If we are still living in the practice of Judaism, it is an admission that we have failed to receive the gift of grace. We have seen how former adherents of the ancient customs and now order their lives by the Lord's day instead (the day when life first dawned for us, thanks to him and his death) . . . To profess Jesus Christ while continuing to follow Jewish customs is an absurdity. The Christian faith does not look to Judaism, but Judaism looks to Christianity, in which every other race and tongue that confesses a belief in God has now been comprehended.

(2) There is one passage in the OT which actually foretold the advent of a new day of worship and praise -

> *The stone that the builders rejected has become the chief corner-stone. This is the Lord's doing, and it is marvellous in our eyes. This is the day that the Lord has made, so let us rejoice and be glad in it* (Ps 118:22-23).

This new day of worship, in which the people of God are to find joy and gladness, is plainly the day of Christ's resurrection, that is, the first day of

---

[27] Hebrew Christians tended to observe the *seventh* day, and Gentile Christians the *first*. These two practices probably arose more from social necessity than from any theological consideration. In the Roman world, Jews were given the special privilege of Sabbath-keeping, but this was not extended to the rest of society. The social condition of many Gentile converts, especially slaves, made Sabbath- keeping impossible.

the week. By his resurrection, Christ has led us into a new sabbath rest, one that is perpetual, not confined to one day a week - *see Hebrews 4:1-10*. Notice how the apostle draws a contrast between the sabbath given to Israel by *Moses*, into which Joshua was unable to lead the people, and the sabbath into which *Christ* leads us. Our sabbath is not found in the observance of a day, but in *"ceasing from our own labours"* so that we can trust in the completed work of Christ. The apostle is emphatic: *"We who believe enter into that rest!"* (vs. 3).

The apostle also points to another passage in the Psalms that predicts the supplanting of the former sabbath with a new day of worship:

> *A long time after Moses God spoke again through David and said, "Today" - just as he had done previously - "Today, when you hear his voice, do not harden your hearts." For if Joshua had given them rest, God would not have spoken later about another day. So then, there remains a sabbath-rest for the people of God* (vs. 7- 9).

This *"sabbath-rest"* of ours is not an occasional thing. It is the continual inner rest faith in Christ brings. It stems from our belief in his glorious triumph over death. We rejoice in the day of his resurrection; indeed, from the very beginning the church has seen the fitness of celebrating the empty tomb by worshipping on the first day of the week.

However, to see the *fitness* of worshipping on a certain day is not the same thing as saying that we are *obliged* to do so; for the fact is -.

WE HAVE NO SACRED DAY

(1) The basic NT position is that no special sanctity is attached to any day whatsoever; we are under no obligation to keep any day holy; there is no fixed sabbath observance for the Christian.

(2) Whatever day we choose for worship is acceptable to God, whether Saturday, Sunday, or any other day. Says Paul -

> *One person values one day above other days, while another esteems all days alike. Let everyone be fully persuaded in his or her own mind* (Ro 14:4-6).

The sole criterion is whether the observance, or non-observance, of a certain day is honouring to God and carried out in love for one's fellow man. In other words, it depends on our ability to do what we do out of faith in God -

> *Whatever your personal beliefs are, keep them between yourself and God. You are indeed fortunate if you find no reason to condemn yourself for the things you approve* (vs. 22).

Paul clarified this principle by using the example of the food laws. He says he will eat only those foods that do not offend a weaker brother (vs. 2,3,6,15,21). In another place he discusses the question of meat offered to idols that was afterward sold in the market. Paul clearly states there is no harm in eating such meat (1 Co 8:7-8); but if doing so would lead a weaker person into idolatry Paul was willing to be a vegetarian for life! (vs. 13). Love for his fellow Christian decided the issue. If an action can be done in love it is good; if not, it is sin. (See also 1 Ti 4:1-5; Mt 7:12).

How then should this principle of love be applied to the sabbath? Simply this: the NT gives no mandate to anyone to demand that the sabbath be kept, or to demand that it not be kept. We are free to observe the seventh day (or any other day) to the glory of God; we are free not to observe it to the glory of God. Paul speaks again -

> *Who gives you the right to pass judgment on someone else's servant? His own master will judge if he stands or falls. And (*a Christian*) will certainly stand, for his Master is able to make him stand* (Ro 14:4).

(3) However, it does appear that many of the first disciples, and the bulk of the church from their day onward, by common consent set aside *Sunday*, the first day of the week, the day on which Christ rose from the dead, as a proper day for worship and praise.

There is much to commend this practice, and Christians should be encouraged to devote this day to the Lord, so long as the encouragement does not sour into a legalistic duty.

The scriptures do oblige the people of God to assemble regularly, at an appointed time and place, for public worship and prayer. In our society, Sunday still provides the most convenient opportunity in which to satisfy that demand. And if the entire day can be spent in godly pursuits, all the better; but no divine law is broken if that is not possible. Yet those who deeply love the Lord will want to spend as much time as possible in preparation for worship, as well as in worship itself. [28]

THE OLD SIGN AND THE NEW

Christians often fail to understand that the sabbath day was given to Israel not merely as a day of rest, but more importantly *as a sign of the covenant relationship* between Israel and God (see Ex 31:12-16). The sign and the covenant are inseparable. Israel's observance of the sabbath signified the nation's acceptance of the covenant, along with the people's willingness to adhere to its terms and conditions. Violation of the sabbath meant rejection of the covenant, and heavy penalties were incurred (Ez 20:12 ff).

But Christ has abrogated the old covenant; it has become obsolete, and has vanished away, and the sign of the sabbath has vanished with it (He 8:13). The collapse of the covenant has made the sign redundant.

The argument here is the same as that applied to circumcision, which was the sign of God's personal relationship with each family in Israel (Ge 17:11-14; Je 4:4; Ex 12:43-38; Ac 7:8; Ro 4:11-12). The ancient rite of physical circumcision has now been replaced by the sign of baptism in water, and the spiritual grace signified by circumcision of the flesh has been realised in a new *"circumcision of the heart"* (see Ro 2:28-29; 4:11-12; Cl 2:11-14; this last reference links circumcision with baptism).

So the ancient sign and the covenant it represented have both vanished, to be replaced by a greater covenant in Christ and a new sign. Christian baptism attests to the inner spiritual grace we have received through the cross of Christ; it shows that we have been *"circumcised in our hearts."*

In the same way, the old sabbath and its associated covenant have been repealed, to be replaced by *"the new covenant,"* a new inner spiritual sabbath-rest, and a new sign, speaking in tongues.

It was not coincidence that the Holy Spirit was given with the sign of glossolalia on the day of Pentecost. The Jewish feast of Pentecost

---

[28] The following references establish our obligation to assemble regularly with the church in worship: Ps 26:8; 27:4; 84:4,10; 122:1; Ep 4:11-13; He 3:13; 10:25; Je 3:15.

celebrated the giving of the law (the Ten Commandments) to Moses on Mt. Sinai. That old law was a gift to Israel, sent down from heaven, amid the glorious fire of God. Sabbath observance was the special sign of Israel's reception of the law. But the Christian Pentecost celebrates the birth of the church, through the heavenly gift of the Holy Spirit, given with fire, and with the new sign of glossolalia.

So Paul, having said that the old covenant has been *"done away"* (including the Ten Commandments), goes on to say that we do not come to a law written on stone, but we come to *"the Lord (who) is the Spirit, and where the Spirit of the Lord is, there is freedom!"* We do not look on the veiled face of Moses, nor do we gaze at tablets of stone, but

> *we all, having our faces unveiled, reflect as in a mirror the glory of the Lord, and we are being transformed into his likeness from glory to glory, which comes from the Lord who is the Spirit* (2 Co 3:17-18).

If it is valid to argue that the sabbath remains, although the thing it signified has vanished, it would be just as valid to argue that circumcision remains although the thing it signified has vanished. The fact is, both arguments are spurious and nullified by the NT. Circumcision and the sabbath were both integral parts and signs of the old covenant. When that covenant was abrogated at Calvary the signs vanished with it.

So we live now under a new covenant, with new grace, and with new signs. To keep the sabbath is as spiritually redundant as to be circumcised.

Paul presents this argument (against circumcision) very pungently in his letter to the Galatians -

> *I, Paul, tell you this: if you accept circumcision, you will no longer gain any benefit from Christ* (5:2).

In the same letter he shows

- ➢ the contrast between the way of *law* and the way of *faith* (3:10-14).
- ➢ that the *"law"* refers primarily to the Ten Commandments given on Mt. Sinai (4:24; and cp. 5:14).

- ➢ that *"circumcision"* simply a metonym for the entire law (including the Ten Commandments, 5:4); hence, if the practice of circumcision is spiritually worthless, so also is keeping the sabbath.
- ➢ that circumcision may be beneficial in some practical and material ways, as also may be the sabbath; but neither can add anything to the righteousness we receive in Christ (6:12-16).
- ➢ that any person who observes any part of the law in order to be justified before God, negates the value of the cross (5:1-12).
- ➢ that God no longer requires us to receive the law, but to receive the Spirit, and that this new heavenly gift is not attested by some human observance but by a supernatural sign (3:2-5,14; 4:6; 5:5).
- ➢ that the observance of special *"days"* is particularly foolish, redundant, even spiritually impoverishing (4:8-11).

There simply is no sound argument to make it mandatory for Christians to observe the sabbath. The other nine commandments, yes, those we must keep, for they are written into the new covenant; but the fourth commandment, no!

CHAPTER EIGHT:

LIBERTY

Where the Spirit of the Lord is, there is liberty . . . and we are being changed into his likeness from glory to glory (2 Co 3:17-18)

St John Chrysostom once preached a passionate sermon on that text to his vast congregation in old Constantinople. Here is part of what he said -

> . . . and like as fire-bright bodies . . . (impart to) those which lie near them . . . somewhat of their own splendour, so truly doth it also happen with the faithful. Therefore surely they with whom it is thus are set free from earth, and have their dreams of the things in the heavens. But woe is me! for well is it that we should here even groan bitterly, for that we who enjoy a birth so noble do not so much as know what is said, because we quickly lose the reality, and are dazzled about the objects of sense. For this glory, the unspeakable and awful, remaineth in us for a day or two, and then we quench it, bringing over it the winter of worldly concerns, and with the thickness of those clouds repelling its rays. For worldly things are a winter, and than a winter more lowering. For not frost is engendered thence, nor rain, neither doth it produce mire and deep swamps; but, things than all these more grievous, it formeth hell and the miseries of hell. And as in severe frost all the limbs are stiffened and dead, so truly the soul, shuddering in the winter of sins also, performeth none of its proper

> functions, stiffened, as it were, by a frost, as to conscience. [29]

How truly the archbishop described our common state. Though we are invited to live by the power of the Holy Spirit, experiencing each day an ever-increasing glory, how quickly we are dazzled by the world! So (as Chrysostom lamented),

> this glory, the unspeakable and awful, remaineth in us for a day or two, and then we quench it, bringing over it the winter of worldly concerns.

One of the great reasons for this frequent spiritual dullness is failure to truly grasp what Paul means when he says, *"where the Spirit of the Lord is, there is liberty!"*

What *liberty* is he talking about?

There are two kinds of liberty: *legal*, and *practical*.

And they follow in that order. Before you can enjoy practical liberty you must first understand your legal liberty. There can be no real freedom in *life* until you know you are free in *law*.

We began to discuss that great truth in your previous chapter. I want to continue the theme here by asking you -

ARE YOU A BIGAMIST?

A *bigamist* [30] is a person who enters into a legal form of marriage while still married to another. In our land the practice is illegal. A divorced or widowed person is free to marry another; but a person whose previous marriage contract is still valid may not lawfully take a second spouse.

In some countries plurality of wives is the accepted custom and missionaries have frequently had to face this problem. There are many

---

[29] The Nicene and Post-Nicene Fathers; Vol 12; St Chrysostom; "Homilies on First and Second Corinthians;" pg. 314; re-printed 1979 by Eerdmans Publishing Co.

[30] Although it has been substantially re-written, this section is based on an article by Leo Harris, in the magazine "Revivalist", August 1970; pg. 5.

stories of missionaries endeavouring to persuade a man to forsake all but his first wife. He usually wishes, since she is probably the youngest and prettiest, to keep only the last one he married!

However, the problem is no less with regard to *spiritual bigamy* - that is, endeavouring to maintain simultaneously two *spiritual* marriage contracts. How is that possible? What are these *"marriages"*? Which one is valid? Which one should be abandoned?

Paul deals with the problem of spiritual bigamy in *Romans 7* -.

AN OBVIOUS PRINCIPLE

> *Surely you are aware, dear friends - for I am speaking to people who know the law - that the law can have authority over you only while you are alive?* (vs. 1)

Paul's point here is simple and obvious. The law applies to a person for his life time only. Death dissolves all legal obligation, and places the dead person beyond the authority or control of the law. The Jews and the Romans both, were proud of their legal codes. The Jews, because their law had a divine origin; the Romans, because their law was the most sophisticated that had yet been invented. But it made no difference. Whether Jew or Roman, death at once nullified the law.

A FAMILIAR ILLUSTRATION

The law says that a married woman is bound to her husband for as long as he still lives; but if her husband dies, then she is discharged from all legal ties to her husband. Therefore, if she marries another man while her former husband is still alive, she will be accused of adultery. But if her husband dies, then she is released from her legal obligation, and she can marry another man without being called an adulteress (vs. 2,3).

Paul uses the familiar example of a marriage to illustrate his principle of death undoing the authority of law. I don't know of any society where the right is denied to a surviving spouse to re-marry after the death of a partner. As the old liturgy expressed it, the wedded couple are bound to each other only "for so long as you both shall live" . . . and . . . "till death us do part." Whether the marriage is happy or miserable, the contract, as far as the law is concerned, is terminated by the death of either spouse.

Notice that Paul calls a woman who is "married to another man" while her first husband is still alive, an adulteress. Legally, today, she would be guilty of bigamy. The word bigamy comes from the Latin bi, meaning two, or twice, and the Greek gamos, which means marriage; hence, contracting two marriages concurrently. But Paul mentions this only because he is about to show how Christians often commit spiritual "bigamy." His purpose, of course, is to teach us how to recognise and avoid this dilemma.

(Let me note in passing, it is unfair to use this passage in an argument about whether divorce and re-marriage are permissible. Paul is not even thinking about those issues in this place; he is simply stating the ordinary rule that the death of a spouse dissolves a marriage and leaves the surviving spouse free to re-marry.)

A STRANGE APPLICATION

Paul applies his lesson about marriage contracts to our relationship with two inseparable foes: *the law of Moses, and sin*. His argument will become clearer if you pause for a few moments and read *Romans 7:7-11*, noting how the law and sin give rise to each other, and how they exercise an implacable tyranny over all who are still wedded to them.

But who *is* wedded to this law/sin slavemaster? We *all* were, until God found a way to release us in Christ. And how did God do that? Paul says

> *Likewise, dear friends, you have become dead to the law through the body of Christ, so that you may belong to another - that is, to him who was raised from the dead - so that you might bear fruit for God* (vs. 4).

All of us were *"married"* to the law of Moses, which had dominion over us as long as we lived. But then Paul makes a startling assertion: this *"marriage contract"* with the law has been dissolved by the death of one of the wedded parties, and the way has been opened for a new *"marriage contract"* to be entered into. Strangely though, Paul says the *believer* is the one who has *"died,"* and also the one who will *"re-marry!"*

That change of direction makes the passage difficult. It would have been much simpler if Paul had written something like this -

> *There was a time when you were married to the Law, a union that caused you untold miseries, leaving you no hope of escape. But then God put Law to death, along*

> *with his offspring Sin, so that now, since your bullying spouse is dead, you are free to marry another, Christ.*

That would seem the logical way to continue his analogy. If all of my sorrows come from my bondage to the Law and Sin, and if God wants to release me from that union, and marry me to another, that is, to Christ, surely the easy solution would be to slay both the law and sin? With the death of my taskmasters I would at once be free to be joined to Christ. Why does Paul surprise us by declaring, not that our dreaded *spouse* has been killed, but that *we* are the ones who must die?

The answer is intriguing and inescapable. It simply was not possible for God to end my marriage to the law by destroying the *law*. Why? Because *"the law is holy, and the commandment is holy and just and good"* (vs. 12). Despite the fact that my misery was caused by the law (because it aroused sin and made me a slave, vs. 7-11), the law itself had not done anything worthy of death. My own sinful nature was at fault, not the law. Furthermore, the law is still the standard by which God judges the world; it is still the measure of his righteousness; it is still the rule by which mankind is required to live. God could not destroy it without in the process destroying his own justice!

So Paul had to make a sudden change of direction. If my wedded bondage to the Law had to be undone, and if the death of one of the spouses was the only remedy, and if the *Law* could not perish, then only one other choice remains: *I* must die! But if I die how then can I be married to another? Am I not dead? Here the marvellous grace and power of the Father are revealed. He found a way in Christ not only to put me to death but to raise me again to life and to *"marry"* me to the living Saviour!

That is why, instead of logically following *verse 2* by declaring that God has put our pitiless *spouse* to death, he suddenly says that God has put *us* to death: *"(So) my brethren, you have died to the law in Christ"* (vs. 4). After all, in relation to a marriage contract, it matters little which spouse dies. In either case, the contract is terminated!

Now notice three things here -

IDENTIFIED WITH CHRIST

We are still looking at *verse 4* of our text (Ro 7:1-6). In this verse Paul reverts to the theme he expounded in his previous chapter: the astonishing concept that the believer has been *crucified with Christ*. This is the great truth known as *identification*. Paul deals with this theme very clearly, stating that believers are -.

- ➢ Baptised into his death (vs. 3)
- ➢ Buried with him by baptism into death (vs. 4)
- ➢ United with him in his death (vs. 5)
- ➢ Crucified with Christ (vs. 6)
- ➢ and so on, throughout the chapter.

Now when Paul says (7:4), *"You have died to the law through the body of Christ,"* he actually uses, in the Greek, the more violent expression, *"You were slain to the law by the (slain) body of Christ."* In other words God reckons us to have been i*dentified* with Christ in his savage death on the cross. When he died, we died.

That is confirmed in *verse 6*, where he says,

> *We are discharged from the law, for <u>we are now dead</u> to the thing that held us captive.*

God is able to reckon us dead through Christ because of the Saviour's total innocence. He was our Surrogate, dying in our place. But how can *one* man die for *many*? How can *all* who believe be accounted as having died with him? Because, being Son of God as well as Son of Man, his life has an infinite value, vastly adequate to encompass the entire human race. Even if the nations were a million times more populous, the life of Christ would be a richly sufficient proxy for them all.

So Paul declares in the clearest possible terms that we who believe have had our relationship to the law dissolved by death; that is, we are counted as having died along with Christ. The immediate result of our *"death"* is to put an end to the old marriage contract. The law and sin still exist (for *they* did not die, *we* did), but we are no longer under contract to them. Their authority over the believer has been nullified.

FREE TO MARRY ANOTHER

Paul does not leave us there, dead. In the sense of the analogy he is using here, we cannot remain in an *"unmarried"* state. So he continues in *verse 4* -

> . . . *that you may be married to a different spouse, that is, to the one him who was raised from the dead, so that we might bear fruit for God.*

Our identification with Christ in his death and resurrection means dissolution of our *"marriage"* to the law and entering into *"marriage"* with Christ in resurrection life and power.

But that leads to a warning -.

BEWARE OF BIGAMY

The burden of Paul's entire argument is this: it is impossible to maintain two legal *"marriages,"* one to the *law* and the other to *Christ*. If you have truly died with Christ, and risen with him, and are now spiritually *"wedded"* to him, it is an act of *"bigamy"* to cling to, or to revive, your former union with the law! Don't be a spiritual bigamist. Have nothing to do with that old spouse. Cling to Christ alone!

That leads to -.

A GLORIOUS RESULT

Two wonderful benefits arise from this dying with Christ, and from coming alive again in him, and being *"married"* to him -

WE ARE RELEASED FROM THE LAW

> *But now, since we are dead to the thing that once held us captive, we are released from the law* (vs. 6).

THE MORAL LAW, OR THE RITUAL LAW?

What *"law"* is Paul talking about when he says that we have *"died"* to the law? He cannot mean *all* law, as though he were saying there are no restrictions of any kind placed upon us Christians, that we can do whatever we like whenever we like. Plainly, all who love the Lord do yearn to do *his* will and to please him with every thought, word, and deed.

We could say that there are two major concepts of *"the law"* threaded through scripture -

First, there is the *general* will of God for his people: that we should walk in holiness, and love, and faith, being obedient to his purpose for each one of us day by day. In that sense of the law, the joy expressed by the psalmist is still echoed by every devout child of God (see Ps 119:10,14,18,33; etc). Which of us can live fruitfully without daily knowledge of the will of God? We certainly have not *"died"* in Christ to *that* law, but rather love it more than ever we did and yearn to bring perfect pleasure to the Father's heart.

Second, there is the law that Moses gave to Israel, with all of its rituals, ceremonies, sacrifices, commandments, oblations, ordinances, and so on. This is plainly the law that Paul is referring to in Romans. It could be summarised as *"any attempt to gain salvation or to earn favour with God by the keeping of a written code."*

But now a question arises: does this ritual law include the famous Ten Commandments? Have we in fact *"died"* to them as well as to the remainder of the Mosaic ordinances?

There are some who agree that the *"law"* to which Paul is referring is the law of ceremonies and rituals established in the Old Testament, but they argue that it does *not* include the *moral law* summed up in the Ten Commandments.

Is that valid?

THE TEN COMMANDMENTS

Let the context clarify the point for us. The law Paul is writing about is that law which he says is contrasted with *grace* (6:14-15). It is the law that brings the knowledge of sin (7:7,9,13). Furthermore, it is the law that says *"you must not covet"* (7:7) - which is, of course, *a direct quotation from the tenth Commandment* (Ex 20:17).

The lesson is inescapable: the law to which Paul says the believer has died is none other than the moral law, that is, the Ten Commandments.

In fact, Paul maintains that *this* (not the ceremonial law) was the very law that *"slew"* us!

> *But when the commandment came, sin revived, and I died* (vs. 9,10). And again: *The very commandment that should have brought me life instead proved to be death for me* (vs. 10). And again: *For sin found an opportunity in the commandment . . . and killed me* (vs. 11).

The question is clearly answered. Do Christians have to keep the Ten Commandments? NO! As far as that written code is concerned, we are like a spouse who has died. We are no longer bound to it. We are no longer under its authority. We are released from it. We are now citizens of a new kingdom, with a new law. We have entered into a contractual union with a new Lord, and we are subject to his law alone.

Once again (see the previous chapter) the problem of the Fourth Commandment is solved. We are not obliged to observe the Sabbath Day, because that was part of the old marriage covenant. We have died to that union, and are bound now only to Christ. He is our one true Husband, our Lord, our Master.

There is a sense, of course, in which every true believer does have been carried over into the New Covenant - yet no longer as the Ten Commandments, but rather as the Law of Christ. If I refrain from coveting my neighbour's wife, it is not because *Moses* so commanded, but because I heed the voice of *Christ*.

Indeed, the law of Christ does not depend upon a written code, because it is spontaneously fulfilled in the believer who *"walks in the Spirit"* and *"bears fruit for God."* Even the Fourth Commandment has found a new dimension - not in the keeping of a particular day, but in the perpetual rest we find in Christ (He 4:9-11). *Every* day for us is a now a sabbath day! We scorn the feeble celebration of but one day a week!

AN ILLUSTRATION

Here is a simple illustration of the principles we are talking about. If you were to migrate to another country you would at once come under the laws of that new land. The laws of your previous country would no longer have any authority over you. How confusing it would be to keep both sets of law at the same time. How foolish to pay taxes to both governments. Of course, you would not do it. It would be quite enough for you to keep the laws and pay the taxes of your new home.

However, it would also be true that many of the laws of your new country would be the same as those of your old. Good law is much the same wherever you go in the world. Some things are forbidden, or required, in every civilised land.

Nonetheless, even if your behaviour in the new land is exactly the same as it was in the old, you are still keeping the *new* laws, not the *old*. You cannot identify the laws you are keeping by the names they had in your former homeland. You must call them by the names they have in your present land.

So with us and the old laws of Moses. Even though some of them are similar to those that belong to the new covenant, we are keeping the new, not the old. We have been shifted from the kingdom of darkness and brought into the kingdom of Christ. We are God's new Israel. We obey *only* the law of Christ.

WHY DO WE NEED TO BE RELEASED FROM THE LAW?

Someone may ask, "Why all this ado about being released from the law? Does it really warrant all this space and effort?"

There are two reasons why you and I should laugh merrily at our discharge from the ancient law -

BECAUSE WE CANNOT KEEP IT

See *Romans 7:21-24*. How pitiful is the state of those who try to gain salvation by keeping the law. Their end can be nothing but despair.

BECAUSE WE CAN KEEP IT

This is a worse state than the first. How delusory law can be. If it fails to destroy you through *despair* it will do so through *pride*. So for every person of tender conscience who, like Paul in *Romans 7:21-24*, weeps in frustration over the way the law foils his every effort to achieve righteousness, there are ten more of shallow heart who are quite persuaded of their own righteousness, and so live in a fool's paradise. Paul talks about such in *Colossians 2:20-23*. They are puffed with pride over their self-denials and their scrupulous taboos, yet they are rotted through with carnality.

The only safe escape from both the despair and the pride that are engendered by law-keeping (when it is practised as a means of salvation), is to flee to Christ, and to be satisfied with him alone as your all-sufficient righteousness.

Happily, in Christ we truly are released from the law, for we have *died* to it, and it no longer has any right or control over us.

But that is only the first benefit of our union with Christ. The second is this -

WE ARE RELEASED FROM SIN

> *While we were controlled by our lower nature, our sinful passions, stirred up by the law, kept on working in our bodies, bearing fruit for death. But now we are discharged from the law . . . so that we no longer serve under the old written code, but in the new way of the Spirit* (Ro 7:5,6).

The *passive* aspect of our union with Christ is that we are discharged from all obligation to the old law; the *positive* aspect, is that we are *released to live victoriously over sin and to be fruitful for God.*

Why then are so many Christians still so defeated? Paul gives the answer in two steps that are required of us -

A CONTINUING ACT OF FAITH

Earlier in his great discourse on law and grace Paul makes this statement

> *You must reckon yourselves to be dead indeed to sin, but alive to God through Jesus Christ our Lord* (Ro 6:11).

"*Reckon yourself*" - that is a faith act. It is a state of mind. It is a constant attitude. It is a spiritual response to the revelation of what God has done for us in Christ. It is a choice you make to believe the word of God, no matter what evidence may seem to belie that word.

And what *should* you "*reckon*" about yourself? Simply that you are *dead* to the law and to sin, but *alive* with Christ!

So there are three stages to this spiritual drama:

- ➤ *first,* by identifying yourself with Christ in his death you do actually die to the law in the heavenly realm, and so the way is prepared for you to live for God

- ➤ *second,* to turn that spiritual reality into victorious daily living, you must constantly and joyfully (despite the evidence of your senses) affirm yourself to be what God says you are in Christ

- ➤ *third,* the result of that *faith-reckoning* will indeed be the conquest of sin, and a life of fruitful Christian service; you will become in *fact* what you reckon yourself to be by *faith.*

But even that may not be enough unless you add a further dimension -

THE NEW LIFE OF THE SPIRIT

To faith must be added the empowering grace of the Holy Spirit -

> *"Walk in the Spirit," said Paul, "and you will not fulfil the lusts of the flesh" (Ga 5:16-24).*

And again,

> *"Where the Spirit of the Lord is, there is liberty. And we all, because our faces are unveiled, are now reflecting the glory of the Lord, and we are being changed into his likeness from glory to glory" (2 Co 3:17-18).*

And again

> *(in our text, Ro 7:6), "We serve . . . in the new life of the Spirit."*

It would be exciting to explore what it means to be carried from *glory to glory* as you live each day filled and controlled by the Holy Spirit. But I cannot do so here.

For now, we need to return to Paul's major theme in *Romans 6 & 7*, which is simply this: *you will never overcome sin until you are cut off from the old law, to which you were wedded, and which gave sin its sting.*

Only as a result of dying to that law, and to sin, and then coming to life again in Christ, and being wedded to him, can you truly escape the old tyranny, coming instead under God's beneficent rule.

Now that brings us back to our starting place - are you a *bigamist*?; that is, are you trying to remain wedded at the same time both to the law and to Christ? How foolish that is, when scripture says you are *"dead to that which held you captive"*, so that now you are *"discharged from the law"* (Ro 7:6).

The word translated *"discharged"* is *katargeo*, which means to make ineffective, powerless, unemployed. The same word is used in *6:6, "So that the sinful body might be destroyed;"* which means the sinful body is made powerless, or rendered ineffective, or inactive. Again, it is found in *1 John 3:8, "For this purpose the Son of God was manifested, that he might destroy the works of the devil."* The works of the devil are still in existence, but they are made powerless, or ineffective, as far as the believer is concerned.

So with the law. It still exists. It applies to every unbeliever in the world. It sets a moral standard by which God will judge all who are outside of Christ. But the believer in Christ is delivered from it - that is, the law has no further power over us, for we have died in Christ.

CHRIST OUR STANDARD

Paul has made it very plain that our union with the law bore *"fruit for death"* (7:5). Our union with Christ, however, should bear *"fruit for God"* (vs. 4).

It is right here that many Christians seem to miss the real significance of Paul's teaching. They fear, if we dissolve our *"marriage"* to the law, we shall have no standard by which to live, and the result will be chaos. They fail to understand the vital reality of our spiritual union with Christ.

That union is not merely an abstract idea, it is a concrete fact. We who believe are indeed powerfully joined to Christ. Consequently, our lives are motivated by the law of faith, the law of love, the law of life - all of which are summed up in the great phrase *the law of Christ* (Ga 6:2).

Christ himself - a living Man, not a written code - is now our standard (Jn 13:34; 15:10-14). We need no other rule. There is no better.

Are you born again? Then you *have* died and risen again in the reckoning of God, and all of the vitality and grace of Christ are freely available to you. You are called to live, not by the rigid demands of commandments carved in stone, not by the old way of the *"letter,"* but by the new way of the Spirit, and by the power of the new life you have in Christ.

So beware of spiritual bigamy. Abandon all thought of maintaining two *"marriage contracts."* Accept your death to the law, and by faith seize all of the benefits of your *"marriage"* with the living Christ. Then you will indeed bear much fruit for God in victorious, successful Christian life.

WHY THE LAW WAS GIVEN

I have been emphasising the dissolution of the old covenant, along with all its law, and the establishment of a new covenant, which is full of abundant grace. And it is perfectly true, if you strive after commandments and law (*"the letter that kills"*), the death of Christ may well become vain for you.

Hence scripture says:

> *No one will ever be justified by doing what the law demands . . . if justification could be gained through the law, then Christ died in vain . . . You will be severed from Christ if you try to find justification through the law; you have fallen away from grace* (Ga 2:16-21; 5:4).

Does the law then, have no value? Most certainly it does!

> *Do we then crush the law by our faith? God forbid! On the contrary, we put the law on a firmer foundation* (Ro 3:31). *And again, The law is holy, and the commandment is holy and just and good* (Ro 7:12).

Why then was the law given? For two reasons: to expose sin; to point to Christ.

THE LAW EXPOSES SIN

When man was created he was made in the image of God (Ge 1:26). He was also made sinless, able to face God fearlessly, and to commune with him. Hence, we read that God issued specific commands to Adam (2:16-17), and in the cool of the evening, God called to Adam to fellowship with him (3:8,9).

However, sin entered the scene, and Adam became ashamed to face his Creator. So he and Eve hid. Their direct fellowship with God was marred, and as a result they were cast out of their beautiful home. Their high calling was disowned, and the gulf between God and man widened. It was not so wide that God could not still speak to man. Even Cain could talk with the Lord (4:9-15). But as generations passed, the gulf widened, and it became ever more difficult to speak with God face to face.

Not only did sin mean less fellowship with God, it also meant less knowledge of the will of God (Ge 6:5,11-12). Nor could the *"fresh start"* in the time of Noah bridge the gulf, and the time came when there was need for a complete re-statement of God's laws in written form, so that all might know the will of God. So the Sinaitic code was given to Moses.

This written law revealed to the world the standards set by God, and showed how far short of those standards man had fallen. This is what Paul meant when he said that through the commandment *"sin became exceedingly sinful";* and again *"the law brought knowledge of sin;"* and, *"sin was indeed in the world before the law was given, but sin cannot be reckoned where there is no law"* (Ro 3:19-20; 5:13; 7:7-14).

It has been said that to know what a house is like you must live in it; to know what love is like, you must love. But that is not so with sin. The person who is <u>most</u> in sin knows <u>least</u> about it! Is not an habitually dirty person less aware of the need for cleanliness? Without some standard, some measure of comparison, sin's power and vileness is unknown by men.

It may be objected, it is promised even of the statutes that, *"those who do them shall live by them"* (Ga 3:12; Le 18:5). Precisely; that is the standard. If you *can* do all those things demanded by the written laws of God, then you will live by them. But the fact is, no man has ever succeeded in maintaining perfect obedience; thus, according to the standards of the law, all the world has become guilty before God (Ro 3:19,23).

So the law exposes sin, and reveals the hopelessness of the human condition.

THE LAW POINTS TO CHRIST

Four hundred and thirty years before the law was given, a promise was made to Abraham and his *"Seed."* This *"Seed"* refers to Christ (Ga 3:16). Thus, before the law was given in written form, there was a promise made, a promise that embraced all mankind - *"In you shall all the nations be blessed"* (3:8). In effect, this promise meant that God would justify the Gentiles by faith, apart from the law, just as he had attributed righteousness to Abraham.

Why then was the law given 430 years later? It cannot, as Paul says, annul the agreement God made with Abraham (3:17). On the contrary, Paul argues that the law was given *to emphasise the promise of faith.* It does that by showing man's inability to save himself, thus demonstrating that salvation can be found only in Christ. In other words, the law was a temporary measure, pending the arrival of that great Son of Abraham to whom the promise was actually made (3:19). It was a kind of tutor, to reveal God's standards, and to show us our desperate need of Christ *until he came* (3:24).

Thus the second purpose of the law is closely related to the first. Because it shows what sin really is, and because it so clearly exposes human weakness, men are forced to realise the need for faith in Christ, Abraham's seed. Thus the law closes itself against man, and compels him to seek righteousness through faith alone. In this way, then, the law actually *supports* faith. Not, as some would have it, by saying, "Keep me, and what your keeping lacks, faith will supply." But rather, "Flee from me altogether, lest I destroy you; be justified exclusively through faith in Christ!"

The argument is summarised by Paul:

> *Does the law then fight against the promises of God? God forbid! For if a law had been given that could impart life, then righteousness would indeed come by the law. But the scripture encloses everybody in sin, so that what was promised to faith in Jesus Christ might be given to those who believe* (3:21-23).

THE NEW LAW OF GOD

An important question now arises: *does liberty mean licence?*

Since we are not under law, can we do as we please, without any fear of the consequences? Hardly!

Let us go back to the illustration of Adam and Eve. Men and women had lost their fellowship with God; thus they needed a written law to show them the standard of life God expected from them, while their human weakness required the law to spell out even minute details.

The NT teaches, however, you can be restored to fellowship with God, and you can know the will of God for your life through your own personal experience and knowledge of God in Christ -

> *Everyone who is led by the Spirit of God is a child of God* (Ro 8:14) . . . *The anointing that you received from him remains in you, so that you do not need anyone to teach you. Rather, as his anointing teaches you about everything, and as it is true teaching and not false, so just as it has taught you, abide in him* (1 Jn 2:27) . . .

> *May you be filled to overflowing with the knowledge of his will in all spiritual wisdom and understanding, so that you may lead a life worthy of the Lord, pleasing him in every way* (Cl 1:9-10; see also Ep 1:17; Ja 1:5).

Thus, by faith you can know once again the position that Adam once knew, of personal relationship and communion with God, and of intimate knowledge of his will. Far from being a life lived on a lower plane than one lived according to the law, this life is lived on a far higher plane. There is no need for instruction by the law, because this life is lived in a realm of sweet fellowship with God, and he personally speaks to and guides his children.

It is clear then, to suggest that abolition of the law will lead to licence is false. Rather, it will open the way for the *letter* to be supplanted by the *Spirit*, and for the fellowship of Eden to be restored!

THE NEW BIRTH

Never forget that the cross has produced two things in us: it crucified us (so that we are dead to the law), and it gave us a new birth (so that we are alive to God) -

> *We know that our old self was crucified with Christ so that our sinful nature might be destroyed, and that we might no longer be the slaves of sin. Anyone who has died is certainly freed from sin! Now if we have died with Christ, we believe that we shall also live with him* (Ro 6:6-8).

That passage highlights the essential meaning of the new birth. Sin and rebellion are the works of the unregenerate life. But that life is now dead. The *"body of sin"* was destroyed at Calvary. Now you are a new creation in Christ, *"dead to sin and alive to God in Christ Jesus"* (vs. 11). Every believer is indwelt by Christ (Cl 1:27), and the life we now live is the result of our faith in him. Christ is our guide, and our strength. He forgives sin and enables us to overcome it. He sets a standard of holiness - himself - and gives us the ability to reproduce his beauty.

> *What a change from the old weak striving after the inflexible and inadequate regulations of the law! Now Christ within us is our helper, and the restorer of more than Adam lost! No wonder Paul exclaimed: "I have*

been crucified with Christ; therefore I no longer live, for it is Christ who lives in me!" (Ga 2:20).

THE LAW OF LOVE

The high plane of life experienced by the Christian is a life lived in love - love for God and for neighbour. This new relationship (as we have seen) arises from the fact that the Christian has died as far as the law is concerned and is now, as it were, married to another, who is Christ. The law has no more power over us than a tyrannical widower has over his deceased wife. We died in Christ, and at once our obligation to the law was broken; we are raised into new life by Christ, so that we might be wedded to him alone.

However, we are not severed from the law in order to remain independent and free to please only ourselves. On the contrary, our severance from the law is followed immediately by union with Christ. The one without the other is impossible. And this union with Christ is one of faith and of love, which provides motivation for a holy life in conformity to the will of God.

Moreover, this new life of love leads to the extraordinary result of actually fulfilling the very law from which we have been severed -

> *Owe no one anything, except a debt of love to each other. If you love your neighbour then you have fulfilled all the law, for the commandments are (all) summed up in this sentence, "You shall love your neighbour as yourself." Love never does any wrong to a neighbour; therefore love is the fulfilment of the law* (Ro 13:8-10).

Therefore, a Christian's motive for conduct is now the *"law of love."* All that we do is now done in a spirit of love to our neighbour. We refuse to steal, not just because it is said to be wrong, but because it is not a fruit of love. So with murder, hatred, disobedience to parents, coveting, adultery, bearing false witness, and so on. These thing are not acts of love, so they cannot be part of a Christian's conduct.

Thus for the Christian the old law in all of its aspects is completely done away, and we have come under a new commandment (Mt 22:37-40; Ro 5:5; 13:8-10; Ga 5:14).

FROM BONDAGE TO LIBERTY

HAGAR AND SARAH

The Bible says that the law means bondage, while faith means liberty (Ga 5:1).

Abraham had two sons. One was born to his wife's slave, Hagar. Her son, Ishmael, was therefore a slave. The other son was born to his wife, Sarah. He, Isaac, was a son indeed. Moreover, Isaac was born when Sarah was well past the age of child-bearing, as a result of a *promise* given *before* the birth of Ishmael (Ge 15:18; 21:1-21). Soon after the birth of Isaac, Ishmael was cast out, so that he might not share the privileges of the true son.

In the New Testament, Hagar, the bondwoman, is said to represent Mount Sinai - from which came the Law. Sarah represents Mount Calvary - from which came grace (Ga 4:22-31).

We too are told to *cast out* the bondwoman and her son, and to *stand fast* in the liberty wherewith Christ has made us *free*, refusing to become entangled again in the yoke of bondage (Ga 5:1). That yoke of bondage is the Law. Its bondage is as miserable as the yoke of any toiling, burden-bearing bullock. Grace, however, is free. Unlike the law, which demands obedience under bondage, grace is the goodness of God toward us when we least deserve it. It means freedom from the power of sin, and from death, the penalty of the Law.

Moreover, we are told that like Isaac, we are sons and daughters of God, not slaves. For God has sent forth the Spirit of his Son into our hearts crying, *"Abba, Father"* (Ga 4:6). The word *Abba* was the Aramaic diminutive used by a young child for *"Father."* It corresponds to our word *"Daddy."* It is a simple expression of faith and trust, and conveys in the deepest sense obedience through sonship and love, not through the rod of the law.

We are told also that through grace we now walk in the Spirit, not the flesh.

The flesh, in the New Testament, stands for self-effort. To walk in the flesh means to walk in our own strength, trusting in our own ability to live rightly. To walk in the Spirit means to walk in the strength of the Holy Spirit, trusting in his ability to make us live rightly (Ro. 8:3-4).

That is the greatest blessing of the Gospel. As well as being born again by the power of God, a Christian can now also know the glory of the Spirit-filled life. It means power (Ac 1:8), overflowing joy (Jn 7:37), love (Ro 5:5), freedom (8:2).

It is a new realm of life, thrilling and challenging far above the dull monotony of a lifeless routine of regulations.

It is a life filled with the supernatural power of God. It brings healing (1 Co 12:9), deliverance in time of distress (Ac 27), and spiritual power (Ac 4).

Are you unsure of your spiritual position? Then be filled with the Holy Spirit, set yourself to walk in the Spirit, and you will know God as never before, and will realise that Christ is the anchor of your soul.

The fruit of the Spirit is love; the fruit of self-righteousness through the law is pride. The Spirit brings abundant, radiant joy; striving after the law brings misery (Ro 7:22-25). The Spirit brings contented peace; the law brings despair and dejection.

The difference is this: walking in the Spirit depends on God's righteousness - which never fails; but walking in the flesh depends on man's righteousness - which always fails.

Therefore,

> *Do not get drunk on wine, and so make yourself wanton. Instead, be filled with the Spirit; speaking to each other in psalms, hymns, and spiritual songs, singing and making melody in your hearts to the Lord. Never stop giving thanks to God the Father for everything, in the name of our Lord Jesus Christ* (Ep 5:18-20).

STAND FAST IN FREEDOM

> *For freedom Christ has set us free; so stand firm, and never again yield your neck to the yoke of slavery* (Ga 5:1).

There we are told that Christ has given us liberty - that is -.

- liberty from the restraint of *Satan*;
- liberty from the restraint of the *law*;
- liberty from the restraint of an *accusing conscience*.

Now, those are legal liberties; they embody what we might call our civil rights as free-born citizens of heaven. We are not slaves, dominated by law, but sons, who live by love. Those liberties are already freely ours in Christ. Those rights and privileges become ours immediately upon our acceptance of Christ.

How is it that so few give evidence of knowing and enjoying these priceless gifts? Because *"Satan has blinded their minds in order to prevent the light of the glorious gospel of Christ from shining upon them."*

Oh! let us come out from under the yoke of bondage, and accept that liberty which is ours in Christ!

Yet we go still further; for all liberty is given that we might be something, or do something. So Paul says that *by the liberty of Christ we find freedom*. That is, when you know your legal rights in Christ, and stand fast in those heavenly privileges, you will be set free. What is this freedom? It has two parts

IT IS FREEDOM FROM -

- the imprisonment of sin, the compulsion of lust, the galling bondage of disease, the thraldom of fear, the authority of Satan; and, in fact, from every *"yoke of bondage!"*

IT IS FREEDOM TO -

- live for God, rejoice in the Lord, pray, believe, strive for a goodly reward.

To have such freedom is to enjoy a liberty scarcely equalled by even that of the holy angels.

But to maintain that freedom you must stand fast in the liberty of Christ.

With deadly hatred Satan has furiously tried to challenge and destroy our Christ-given liberty and the freedom we can find thereby.

That is why many people find it so difficult to maintain their liberty and freedom. Hence the feeling of vehemence about the apostle's words! We *must* stand fast!

But is it not worth every effort?

Energetically stand your ground! Steadfastly maintain your rights in Christ! Don't be negligent or slothful or careless in guarding your immense privileges!

Nor is that difficult to do. It requires only that you

UNDERSTAND

Thoroughly instruct yourself in your gospel liberty, so that you will be prepared in the day of temptation, and can unwaveringly stand your ground against the blandishments and accusations of Satan.

It is not possible to stand fast in something of which we are ignorant. We must fully *understand* before we can *stand*!

BELIEVE

Wax bold in faith, claiming with all zeal and confidence the liberty and deliverance which are yours in Christ, holding up the rights you have as freeborn children of God.

Steadfastly refuse to allow Satan to falsely entangle you again in any yoke of bondage.

Let us live in the freedom for which Christ has set us free, each day advancing from glory to glory as we walk in the Spirit by faith!

ADDENDUM ONE:
THE PIERCED EAR

Joseph ben Azar was a slave. [31]

Six years earlier, overwhelmed by debt, he had been forced to sell himself to rich old Ahud, the lord of the whole valley. Joseph's servitude had been mild (for Ahud was a kindly man) but even so the labor was long; and there was nagging shame in being a bondman (he who had once been free) and in knowing that his children shared his humiliation.

The law said that every Hebrew slave should go free after six years of service, and that the master should provide his former servant with sufficient goods to re-establish himself as a self-supporting citizen -

> *If one of your fellow Hebrews, whether a man or a woman, is sold to you, he or she shall serve you for six years, then in the seventh year you must set the slave free. You must also provide generously for the freed person, with gifts from your flocks, your threshing floor, and your winepress. . . . You must let your slave go free from you without resentment, for at half the cost of a hired servant your slave served you for six years. If you do this, the Lord your God will bless you in everything you do* (De 15:12-18).

The sixth year of Joseph ben Azar's bondage was now ended, but Ahud had not yet released him, he was still a slave. Why?

---

31 This chapter gives a picture of justification from a different viewpoint. It is taken from a magazine article I wrote some years ago.

PERHAPS JOSEPH WAS IGNORANT OF THE LAW

That situation often arose in ancient Israel. The people were usually illiterate, and the rich slave owners frequently made sure their captives heard nothing about the law of release. So, men and women who should have gone free after six years of service remained in bondage all of their lives.

Now there is a picture here of many Christians. The Bible says we were all sold into slavery to sin and Satan; but Christ came to create for every Christian a *year of release*. Jesus himself declared -

> *God has anointed me to preach deliverance to the captives, and to proclaim the Lord's year of Jubilee* (Lu 4:18- 19).

The phrase *"the Lord's year of Jubilee"* is a direct reference to the old year of release, when every Hebrew slave was to be set free. But now, under the new proclamation of the gospel, every Christian has become a freeborn child of God, with abundance given to them to establish a new life in the liberty of Christ.

But despite this great act of God, the devil still endeavours to imprison us in two ways -

BY KEEPING US IGNORANT OF THE LAW

The slave who does not know that his term of servitude has ended, that in the eyes of the law he is now a free man, will be content to remain in chains. But let him understand his true legal status and he will at once loudly demand his rights and refuse to serve his former master.

So must you realise that Christ has *already* established the year of release. You are living in it right now! Legally you are free! Satan is no longer your rightful lord, nor sin your rightful master. Refuse to serve them again! (See Ro 6:6-14).

BY RE-TAKING HIS SLAVES AFTER THEY HAVE BEEN RELEASED.

It sometimes happened in Israel that slave owners gave lip service to the law by releasing their slaves on the last day of the sixth year, only to clamp the fetters once more upon their wretched captives a few days later, and compel them to continue in labor.

Jeremiah tells of one occasion when that happened (Je 34:8-11). He pronounced an awful vengeance on the nation and rebuked them mightily with the word of the Lord (vs. 12-17).

Likewise, most Christians find that Satan endeavours to re-impose his will upon them and to lure them again into captivity; but our answer lies in the same weapon used by the prophet - the word of God. That sharp sword the devil can't abide! (Ep 6:11,17).

PERHAPS JOSEPH DIDN'T BELIEVE THE GOOD NEWS

The law of release was so unlike the statutes of every other nation that many people in ancient Israel refused to take it seriously. The rich and powerful laughed it away. The slaves hardly dared to believe it, and they were rarely bold enough to assert their rights.

Many Christians today are in exactly the same position. Crushed by the evidence of their servitude, fearful of the power of the oppressor, they cannot believe that in reality Christ has set them free! They see only the chains that appear to hold them as firmly as ever; they can feel only the lash of temptation, the galling bondage of sin, or the pain of their disease. They groan and abandon hope.

But my friend, freedom depends on knowing the truth that you are already free in Christ. The year of release is here now! Christ says to you

> *Know the truth, and the truth will make you free . . . If the Son makes you free, you will be free indeed!* (Jn 8:32,36). And Paul urged: *Stand fast therefore in the freedom for which Christ has made you free, and do not submit your neck again to the yoke of bondage!* (Ga 5:1).

Believe it, friend! You have slaved long enough! The law of God says you are free: free from the authority of sin, of sickness, and of Satan. Stand on that law; demand your rights; bring the strength of the Word of God against your oppressor; and you will certainly prevail and gain your liberty!

PERHAPS JOSEPH WAS AFRAID OF THE OUTSIDE WORLD

It sometimes happened that a slave would refuse to accept liberty, even when it was offered to him by a God-fearing master, because he feared the demands of living as a free man. Although it meant humiliation and drudgery, he preferred to remain a slave, with no responsibility, able to depend on his master for the bare necessities of life.

Understand this: *a pre-requisite for freedom is always to love it passionately*. But there are still many who, deep at heart, prefer bondage. We meet them all the time:

- ➤ alcoholics and drug addicts who fail to respond to prayer simply because they are afraid to face life, their problem gives them an excuse for failure;
- ➤ or sick people, who seek healing but don't find it because actually they don't want it - they would like to be rid of the pain of their affliction, but they enjoy the sympathy, attention, and seclusion it brings them, and they don't really want to get well;
- ➤ or smokers, who remain chained to their habit because they can't bear to lose the comfort and relief they imagine it brings them;
- ➤ or sinners, who never master their sin because deep inside they love it too much;
- ➤ and so on.

Know this: *you are unlikely to be free unless you want freedom more than anything else on earth*! If you are content to remain bound, the Tempter will be content to hold you in bondage. But if you insist on liberty you will find it, for Christ has already written your release!

PERHAPS JOSEPH LOVED HIS MASTER TOO DEARLY TO LEAVE HIM

Moses spoke about this in his original law of release -

> *Sometimes, because they are happy in your service, and love you and your family, your slaves may say to you, "I do not want to be set free." Then you may take an awl,*

> *and drill through the slave's ear into the door, and for the rest of his or her life that person will remain your slave* (De 15:16-17).

When a slave prospered in his master's service, and reached a high position in his household, to leave it would be folly - he could not possibly do so well by himself. In such cases the slave often swore fealty to his master forever, declaring it publicly by suffering a hole to be bored in his ear.

Now an extraordinary fact comes to light. The Bible describes Christ as *a slave with his ear bored!*

> *Sacrifice and offering you did not desire, but <u>you have pierced my ears</u>* (Ps 40:6); *and again, The Lord God has <u>pierced my ear</u>, and I was not rebellious* (Is 50:5, literal).

What does that mean? Simply, the only way Christ could release us from bondage was to make himself a slave and to humble himself to the degradation and anguish of the cross (Ph 2:6-8). He tasted the bitterness of lash, spike, insult, and blow. But now, having shaken off those appalling fetters in his glorious resurrection, he is exalted again to his Father's right hand; and to him is given power and authority to make us magnificently free!

But those who would know the fellowship of this Son who became a slave, must themselves become slaves that they may be his sons! He said,

> *Take my yoke upon you and be taught by me . . . for my yoke is easy, and my burden is light (Mt 11:28-30).*

But those who truly know him, and love his service, know also that *"he fares well"* with those who are in his house. They are glad for their ears to be pierced to his door.

Christ loved you, and gave himself for your release. His ear was pierced. How about yours?

ADDENDUM TWO:

THEORIES OF ATONEMENT

I have indicated in various places in this book that no one theory of salvation can satisfy all that the scripture says on the subject. Rather the Bible uses many different methods, approaches, illustrations, analogies, metaphors, in its attempt to explain the wonderful thing God has done for us in Christ.

For that reason, theologians encounter great difficulty when they try to construct a theory of salvation that contains all that scripture teaches, yet does so without inner contradictions, or without one theory trespassing on or offending another.

Nowhere is the problem more acute [32] than in the matter of explaining the *atonement*. The following comments may be of interest to you. They are taken from the article *"Atonement"* in *"The New International Dictionary of the Christian Church"*. [33]

The Christian Church has never accepted any one way of viewing the Atonement as the orthodox way. The result is that there are many ways in which Christians have answered the question, *"How does the death of Christ long ago and so far away save me here and now?"* We can detect three broad trends in the multiplicity of theories of atonement thrown up during nineteen centuries of church history.

---

[32] Acute, that is, to western theologians, who demand self-consistent and sequential logic in all of their thinking. The biblical authors carried no such burdens, and mixed their metaphors and confused their analogies with a cheerful disregard for our modern, western prejudices.

[33] General Editor, J. D. Douglas; Paternoster Press, Exeter, Great Britain; 1974, pg. 83. This is a concise yet comprehensive reference work; a valuable tool for any serious student of the church.

The first trend is seen in what Gustav Aulen has called the *"classic"* or *"dramatic"* view. It leans heavily on those biblical passages which speak of the Atonement as a ransom. It sees sinners as justly belonging to Satan because of their sin. But in the death of his Son God paid the price of their redemption. Satan accepted Jesus in place of sinners but he could not hold him. On Easter Day Jesus rose triumphant, leaving Satan without both his original captives and their ransom. Aulen . . . sees the essence of the Atonement as a process of victory over all the forces of death and evil. Most agree that victory is important, but they do not see this as the whole story.

The second group of theories may be said to have originated with Anselm, who saw sin as dishonour to the majesty of God. On the cross the God-man rendered satisfaction for this dishonour. Along similar lines the Reformers thought that Christ paid the penalty sinners incurred when they broke God's law. The strong points of this theory are its agreement with biblical teaching (eg. on justification) and its insistence that the moral law cannot be disregarded in the process of forgiveness.

The third group of theories (especially linked with the name of Abelard) sees the Atonement in the effect on man of what Christ did. When we contemplate the love of God shown in the death of his Son we are moved to repent and to love him in return. We are thus transformed. All is subjective.

All three theories have something to say to us. Each is inadequate by itself (especially the third, for it sees Christ as doing nothing except setting an example, the real salvation is worked out by sinners themselves). But taken together they help us to see a little of Christ's great work for men.

BIBLIOGRAPHY

Believer's Bible Commentary; William Macdonald; Thomas Nelson Publishers, 1989.

Bible Background Commentary; Intervarsity Press, Nottingham UK, 1993.

Bible Knowledge Commentary, The; by John Walvoord and Roy Zuck; Cook Communications, Colorado Springs, Colorado, 1989.

Calvin's Commentaries; John Calvin (1509-1564).

Canterbury Tales; tr. by Nevill Coghill, Penguin Books, 1977.

Christianity Today, art. Feb 6th, 1981.

College Press NIV Commentary, The; Joplin, Missouri, 1996.

Commentary on Ephesians, A; Charles Hodge (1797-1878).

Commentary on the Bible; Adam Clarke (1715-1832).

Commentary On The Old And New Testaments, A; John Trapp (1601-1669).

Commentary on the Old and New Testaments, A; Robert Jamieson, A. R. Fausset, David Brown, 1871.

Death of an Expert Witness; by P. D. James.

Explanatory Notes on the Whole Bible; John Wesley (1703-1791).

Exposition of the Entire Bible; John Gill (1690-1771).

Expositor's Bible Commentary, The; ed. Frank E. Gaebelein; Zondervan Publishers, Grand Rapids, Michigan.

Expository Commentary; H.A. Ironside (1876-1951).

Hastings' Dictionary of the Apostolic Church; Baker Book House, Grand Rapids, 1973.

Holman New Testament Commentary; ed. Max Anders; B & H Publishing Group, Nashville, Tennessee, 2004.

Interpreter's Bible, The; Abingdon Press, New York, 1952.

IVP New Testament Commentary Series, The; Intervarsity Press, Nottingham, UK.

Jewish New Testament Commentary; David H. Stern; Jewish New Testament Publications, Inc., Clarksville, Maryland, 1982.

Knowing The Doctrines of the Bible, by Myer Pearlman; Gospel Publishing House, Springfield, USA. 1937.

Man In Christ, A; by James Stewart; Hodder & Stoughton, London, 1972,

Matthew Henry's Commentary; Marshall, Morgan, and Scott, London, 1953.

Matthew Poole's Commentary; 1685

Nelson's New Illustrated Bible Commentary; Thomas Nelson Inc., New York, 1999.

New Bible Dictionary; I.V.F., London, 1967.

New International Dictionary of the Christian Church, The; General Editor, J. D. Douglas; Paternoster Press, Exeter, Great Britain, 1974.

New Testament Commentary; Baker's Publishing House, Grand Rapids, Michigan, 1987.

Notes on the Bible; Albert Barnes (1798-1870).

People's New Testament Commentary, The; B. W. Johnson; Word Search Corporation, Nashville, Tennessee, 2010.

People's New Testament, The; by B. W. Johnson, 1891.

Poor Man's Commentary On The Whole Bible, The; Robert Hawker, 1850.

Preacher's Commentary, The; Word Inc., Nashville, Tennessee, 1992.

Preacher's Outline and Sermon Bible; Word Search Corporation, Nashville, Tennessee, 2010.

Pulpit Commentary, The; ed. Joseph S. Exell, Henry Donald Maurice Spence-Jones, 1881.

Vincent's Word Studies; Marvin R. Vincent, 1886

Wiersbe's Expository Outlines; Warren W. Wiersbe; Publisher, David C. Cook, Colorado Springs, Colorado.

Word Pictures In The New Testament; A. T. Robertson, 1933.

www.ingramcontent.com/pod-product-compliance
Lightning Source LLC
Chambersburg PA
CBHW071712090426
42738CB00009B/1745